America's
Most Influential
First Ladies

America's
Most Influential
First Ladies

Carl Sferrazza Anthony

Foreword by Betty Ford

illustrated with photographs

The Oliver Press, Inc.
Minneapolis

The Oliver Press
Josiah King House
2709 Lyndale Avenue South
Minneapolis, MN 55408

Library of Congress Cataloging-in-Publication Data

Anthony, Carl Sferrazza.
America's most influential first ladies / Carl Sferrazza Anthony ;
foreword by Betty Ford.

p. cm. — (Profiles)
Includes bibliographical references and index.
   Summary: Examines the contributions and accomplishments of
eleven presidential wives: Dolley Madison, Mary Lincoln, Nellie Taft,
Florence Harding, Eleanor Roosevelt, Jacqueline Kennedy, Lady Bird
Johnson, Pat Nixon, Betty Ford, Rosalynn Carter, and Nancy Reagan.
ISBN 1-881508-00-5 : $14.95

1. Presidents—United States—Wives—Biography—Juvenile litera-
ture. [1. First Ladies.] I. Title. II. Series: Profiles
(Minneapolis, Minn.)
E176.2.A57 1992
973'.099—dc20   92-18444
[B]   CIP
                                                     AC

ISBN 1-881508-00-5
Profiles II
Printed in the United States of America
99 98 97 96 95 94 93 92   8 7 6 5 4 3 2 1

Contents

Newlyweds Betty and Gerald Ford celebrate their marriage during the 1948 congressional campaign. Thus began the Fords' public life in Washington that culminated in the White House.

Foreword

Throughout the history of our great nation, the women who have served as our first ladies have filled that role in many different ways. The first lady has been an elegant hostess, an advisor on new ideas in public policy, the quiet supporter of her husband, and the outspoken supporter and advocate for controversial causes. Our first ladies have worked both quietly and forcefully for the things they believed were important.

Being first lady is a demanding position and a very great honor. When Gerald Ford and I exchanged wedding vows on October 15, 1948, I never imagined what would ultimately result of marrying the man of my dreams. Being first lady was hard work, but I enjoyed every minute of it.

Betty Ford

Author's Note

Although referring to the first ladies and the presidents by their first names may seem informal, the author decided that this was preferable to calling them "Mrs." and "Mr." throughout each life story.

Above all, first ladies and presidents are human beings. In private, they usually called each other by their first names. So, in writing about both their public and their private lives, calling them by their first names seemed appropriate.

Introduction

*I*n 1789, when Congress decided that George Washington should become the first president of the United States, nobody thought about what his wife Martha would do. Would she work like her husband? Was she allowed to speak out on governmental issues? When he had special meetings or parties with important men should she also be there? Should she be in charge of the food, the music, the servants? What if some people needed her help with their problems—was she allowed to help them? Could she talk to the president and other men who could help people with problems? Should she be treated differently from other women?

There were many questions, and no answers. Martha Washington acted carefully. In her day, few women went to school and learned the same things men were taught. Martha was not trained for questions of government. However, she had come from a wealthy

Martha Custis (1732-1802), a widowed mother of two (two others had died as babies), married George Washington in 1759. George and Martha Washington had no children together.

Virginia family and knew how to manage a plantation and take care of the many guests who came to stay there, sometimes for weeks. So, as the president's wife, Martha made sure that guests and visitors of the president were looked after, that the house in which she and the president lived was run properly, that she dressed in formal clothes to give a presidential appearance, and that the food and drink were always the best. Martha Washington was an outstanding hostess.

The second president's wife was different. Unlike Martha Washington who came from the South where culture was based on agriculture, Abigail Adams was from New England. There her intelligent grandfather and father educated her in their library. Government and politics interested Mrs. Adams more than entertaining and fashion. So as the second president's wife, she shared her opinions with her husband just as she had always done. She talked about politics and current events with other men. Even the newspapers and ordinary citizens knew about her involvement in politics.

Since 1800, the presidents and their families have lived in the White House in Washington, D.C. Martha Washington did not live there because construction was completed only after George Washington's term as president was over. Anna Harrison, married to William Henry Harrison, the tenth president, did not live in the White House because her husband died as president in just one month, before she could travel the winter roads to get to Washington from their home in Ohio. Except for those two presidents' wives, however, 35 wives have lived in this house on Pennsylvania Avenue in Washington, D.C.

Every president's wife is different, and they have come from all parts of the United States: New England, the Mid-Atlantic, the South, the Midwest, and the West. One was not even born in America. Their fathers had many different occupations—lawyers, judges, ministers, starch makers, businessmen, shoemakers, traveling salesmen, general store owners, miners, and bankers. A few of them also had mothers who worked outside the home as, for example, teachers, nurses, actresses and managers. Depending on what was considered the best way for a girl to become a woman in each different period of history, the presidents' wives were educated in different ways—from reading in a library like Abigail Adams, to being taught in public schools and private schools, attending high school and college. Depending on their interests and what was considered the proper kind of work in different periods of history, the presidents' wives have had many kinds of jobs before and after they were married: farm manager, schoolteacher, bank clerk, jewelry store owner, artist, newspaper manager, geologist, writer, journalist, public speaker, editor, model, actress, beauty shop assistant, factory worker, and dancer.

Nobody knows exactly where the title "first lady" comes from, but the American people always called Martha Washington "Lady Washington." Seventy years later, in 1860, America had a president who was not married, James Buchanan. He had raised his young niece, Harriet Lane, like a daughter. She wasn't a president's wife, so one newspaper, Frank Leslie's *Illustrated Newspaper,* called her "first lady." The title became popular, and when a male president's wife, daughter, sister, or niece serves as his hostess, she is called the "first lady."

The wives of four of our presidents—Thomas Jefferson, Andrew Jackson, Martin Van Buren, and Chester Arthur—died before their husbands went to the White House. The wives of three presidents—John Tyler, Benjamin Harrison, and Woodrow Wilson—died in the White House. However, since Tyler and Wilson remarried while in the White House, they each had two first ladies.

The things a president's wife does make up her

"role." A first lady's role may be defined two ways: the first lady is usually like most women of her period; often she has the same views and outlook as her countrywomen. So, in one way, her role is based on what is expected of any woman of the time. As Martha Washington did, however, the individual first lady decides what she will or will not do. So, in another way, the first lady does what most interests her and what she feels she can do best.

When first ladies first come to the White House, many are not sure what to do. On the one hand, the first lady is not elected to an official role. On the other hand, her fame can bring the world's attention to social problems. Thus, besides being hostess, Martha Washington was known for her concern about the welfare of men who had been soldiers in the Revolutionary War. So, from the beginning, the president's wife has usually had a special cause for which she is known.

To this day, the United States government has no rules about what a first lady must do. However, as the last two hundred years have passed, Americans have seen more of the first ladies. They have seen her greet groups visiting the White House, help a charity, set an example during a time of national crisis, travel with—and sometimes without—her husband, meet with other political leaders to push for legislation. Today, the American public expects a first lady to do something for the good of humankind, and all the modern first ladies have done so in their area of interest.

In the past, when women were not allowed to be openly involved in politics, first ladies often kept their roles secret. Because they were not sure how the American public and the newspapers would react to their activities, they seldom revealed just how much they helped the presidents and contributed to the country. Even Rutherford Hayes, who was president from 1877 to 1881, once joked that "Mrs. Hayes may not have much influence with Congress, but she has a lot of influence with me." Since 1920, when women were given the right to vote, most first ladies have talked more about their roles and done more public activities. Florence Harding, who was first lady from 1921 to 1923, even wrote that someday in the future women

Angelica Singleton (1817-1878) met her future father-in-law, President Martin Van Buren, in 1837 at a White House dinner arranged by her cousin, Dolley Madison. When Angelica married Van Buren's son, Abraham, she became the widower president's official hostess.

From a wealthy and prominent New York family, Julia Gardiner (1820-1889) married President John Tyler, 30 years her senior, in 1844, just eight months before he left office. Tyler married Julia less than two years after his first wife, Letitia, died in the White House.

might earn more money than their husbands and that this would be acceptable.

During the 1970s, the national movement for women's equality was joined by First Lady Betty Ford. Since that time, the national press and the American public have come to accept a first lady talking about politics. Rosalynn Carter, who was first lady from 1977 to 1981, had this to say about being first lady: "As the role of American women changes, so, too, does the role of first lady."

Universally respected and admired, Dolley Madison became the role model for White House hospitality to which future first ladies would be compared.

1

Dolley Madison

Martha Washington had been a good hostess, and Abigail Adams had been a good politician, but neither of them had ever felt comfortable with the idea of being a public figure. When Martha took her grandchildren to a wax museum, she was noticed by the public. When Abigail went to the theater and cried, the newspaper reported the occurrence. Martha said she felt like "a state prisoner," and Abigail said she was "sick, sick, sick of public life." But when Thomas Jefferson became president in 1801, a new type of first lady came to the White House—a public first lady. Her name was Dolley Madison.

Jefferson's wife had died 20 years before, his two daughters lived in Virginia with their families, and the wife of his vice-president had also died. After the vice-president, the second most important advisor to the president in what is called the cabinet is the secretary of state. So Jefferson turned to the wife of Secretary of State James Madison to help him entertain women guests. Thus, Dolley Madison's public life began. As a young Quaker girl growing up dressed in gray, she could never have imagined for herself this kind of life.

Dolley was born on May 20, 1768, in North Carolina. Her parents, John Payne and Mary Coles, were Quakers, members of a religious sect that believed in peace, a full education for women, and the abolition, or end, of slavery. (Slavery had begun in the colonial period in the United States.) As part of their vow to Quakerism, the Paynes freed their slaves and moved to the city of Philadelphia, where many Quakers lived.

Moving to the city was exciting for 15-year-old Dolley. "I saw more people in my first half hour in Philadelphia," she said, "than I had in my whole life." As a young girl in Philadelphia, Dolley Payne dressed in the traditional gray gown and cap of the Quakers. Although many different types of people filled the city, the Philadelphians often ridiculed the Quakers because of their dress and customs. In school, Dolley received an education like a boy's, including language, math, and philosophy.

When she was 21 years old, Dolley Payne married a Quaker lawyer, John Todd. Working as a law assistant for her husband, Dolley helped to keep his papers in order. As she did this, Dolley's mother inspired her. Mrs. Payne shared equally with her husband in the responsibilities of supporting their family. She had also

This is how Philadelphia looked to the young Dolley Madison.

been given the job of chief clerk in their Quaker meetinghouse. When Mr. Payne died and left no money, Mrs. Payne supported herself by opening a boardinghouse. Many of the boarders were congressmen who lived in Philadelphia because it was the capital of the United States. (New York had been the first capital.)

Without warning, a disease called yellow fever, carried by mosquitoes, hit the city of Philadelphia. Suddenly, Dolley Payne Todd's life changed forever. Her husband, mother-in-law, father-in-law, and one of two sons died within three and one-half weeks.

In order to get her fair share of her husband's property, the widow Todd had to fight her husband's brother in court. Congressman Aaron Burr, one of the boarders in her mother's home, became her lawyer, and she received her correct share. Burr also introduced her to a

Virginia congressman who was many years older than she, and many inches shorter. Such differences didn't matter, however, for soon Dolley Todd and James Madison grew to love each other.

Ever since she was a child, people had noticed that Dolley had a joy of life and a curiosity about things and people who were different from her. She had black hair and blue eyes, a wonderful sense of humor, and a quick wit. This strong personality appealed to most people who came in contact with her. Congressman Madison must have perceived this spirit under the gray Quaker clothes she wore, for he wanted to share his life with her. Dolley agreed to marry him in 1794. However, she held onto the property she had inherited from her first

Aaron Burr (1757-1836) served his country both militarily and politically, rising to the vice-presidency in 1801. He also acted as matchmaker for Dolley and James Madison.

husband, because it would provide her with some independent income. She did not want to become dependent. "There is one secret," Dolley once said, "and that is the power we all have in forming our own destinies."

The former Quaker was now Mrs. Madison. Dressed in fashionable silks and glittering jewelry, Dolley felt her spirit blossom. As a congressman's wife, however, she did more than dress well. She became involved in serious political conversations. Using her sense of humor and kindness, she helped the guests who did not agree with Madison's politics to understand her husband's opinion. When Congressman Samuel Dexter, for example, argued during the day with Madison, Dolley invited him to dinner at night and was able to quiet his anger at her husband.

In 1801, when Thomas Jefferson became the third president and moved into the new White House in Washington, D.C. (the third capital), he invited his friends, the Madisons, to live with him until they bought a home of their own. As President Jefferson's official hostess, Dolley Madison quickly became popular: She led a drive to collect the essentials needed by Lewis and Clark for their exploration of the Louisiana Territory. She stopped entertaining during the Barbary wars. At a Fourth of July picnic on the White House lawn, she joked that she was "amusing myself with the mob." Whenever separated from her husband, she wrote him for political information so she could stay informed.

Dolley Madison's interest in politics was not like that of Abigail Adams, who served as an advisor to her husband. Instead, the people who worked in politics interested Dolley. She was friendly with all politicians, even if they had different views from her and her husband. What made her a political first lady was that her popularity influenced the way people thought about her husband. After Jefferson's two terms as president, James Madison ran for president himself. When Madison won, Charles Pinckney, his political opponent, said he was "beaten by Mr. and Mrs. Madison. I might have had a better chance had I faced Mr. Madison alone." In 1809, on her first day as first lady, Dolley Madison showed how she was able to use her social skill for political purposes. At that time England and France were at war with each other. The representatives of both countries came to the inaugural ball, the large dance and dinner party held to celebrate the day a new president starts his job. Instead of sitting with one representative or the other, Dolley Madison sat down between the two of them, thus pleasing both.

Dolley Madison loved the public. They sent her gifts, like a tiger skin, asked her to endorse books, and wrote her just to keep her informed of news in their hometowns. They called her "Lady Madison" or "The Presidentress." Her face appeared on the cover of a magazine, a line of boats was named for her, and even a dance song, "Mrs. Madison's Minuet," was written in her honor. Friendly with reporters, Dolley was never shy about talking with them for their newspapers. Her custom of serving ice cream at her parties helped make the dessert popular in the United States.

Dolley Madison practiced the idea of democracy for

The fourth president of the United States, James Madison (1751-1836) knew he had a strong political ally as well as mate, in his wife Dolley.

all people. She welcomed everyone, not just the wealthy and politically important, to the White House. When two elderly ladies from the West came to the White House one day to see her, Dolley interrupted her breakfast with the president and gave them kisses, which was all they wanted. She was friends with some Roman Catholic nuns who lived in nearby Georgetown, as well as with the first Jewish diplomatic representative, Mordecai Noah, and she attended different kinds of religious services. For children, she began the Easter egg roll contest on the lawn of the Capitol building. Her most famous innovation was the "Wednesday Night" party where food was served and all the public—

no matter what they did or what they looked like—were welcomed. Everyone from writers, actors, and inventors, to Native American chiefs attended. When someone told her that "Everybody loves Mrs. Madison," Dolley's answer described her role as she saw it: "Mrs. Madison loves everybody."

Dolley Madison often wore turbans from Paris with long colored bird feathers and used rouge on her cheeks. But the public didn't care how she looked, they were impressed by how she treated them. She appeared like royalty, but Congressman Mitchell of New York expressed how everyone felt about Dolley when he called her the "Queen of Hearts."

Repeatedly, Dolley's personality helped her husband politically. When two congressmen were feuding and threatening to fight a duel, she brought them together and helped them to settle their differences. She became good friends with Henry Clay, an important young congressman from the West. Clay was the leader of "The War Hawks." This group of western congressmen wanted America to go to war with England, which was capturing American ships and taking American sailors prisoner. Because of Dolley's friendship, the War Hawks gave their political support to President Madison when he ran for a second term. Senator Pope, an opponent of Madison, joked that Dolley herself made "a very good president, and must not be turned out."

After being re-elected, Madison declared war on England in 1812. During the War of 1812 he told his wife all the secret war news, and she kept this information to herself. When the authorities threw the son of a

Quaker friend into prison because his religion did not permit him to fight, she arranged for his release. As a Quaker, Dolley believed that war should not be fought, but she also believed that a country should defend itself when attacked. After American troops led by Henry Dearborn burned some of the government buildings in Canada, which was allied with England, British soldiers and sailors landed in the United States and threatened not only to burn Washington but to take the first lady prisoner and bring her to London, the capital of England.

In the White House, Dolley kept a sword nearby and remained strong. She made speeches to encourage soldiers. When both the president and his assistant became sick, the first lady took over some of their work. She became good friends with William Henry Harrison, an American general, and even sent secret information from the War Department to support him when a governor questioned his ability. One famous legend about Dolley Madison is that she suggested to the president that he give permission to Francis Scott Key to board a British ship so he could try to get a prisoner released. Madison did so, and while on the British ship, Key wrote the poem that became the "Star-Spangled Banner," later the national anthem of the United States.

On the hot day of August 24, 1814, the British invaded Washington. Because the president was with the American troops, Dolley was alone in the White House. She kept running to the roof with her binoculars to see if the British were approaching. When a messenger arrived and told her she was in great danger, Mrs.

Madison refused to leave the White House without taking with her a famous painting of George Washington and a batch of important documents. Because the frame of the painting was screwed to the wall and removing it would take too long, Dolley Madison ordered that the frame be broken. She also decided to take a painting of herself. Only then did she run from the White House, disguised as a farmer's wife. Not long after, the British burned the White House and other government buildings.

Afterward, many people thought that the government should return to its second capital, Philadelphia. However, Dolley Madison, believing that rebuilding Washington was a sign of strength, influenced her husband against the decision to leave. Instead, the Madisons moved into the Octagon House, a private home with eight sides. There the president signed the peace treaty ending the war. That night, Dolley held one of her most famous parties and was described as being "the observed of all observers." Because of the War of 1812, Dolley Madison became a national legend, and some soldiers even gave her the flag of a captured British ship.

Before she left Washington, Dolley Madison became involved in a special project for young orphan girls. She helped organize a group of women in Washington who gathered money to build an orphans' home, cut some of the clothes for the orphans with her own scissors, and even donated $20 (a large sum of money at that time) and a cow to the orphanage.

Mrs. Madison was a woman with strong opinions. She believed that women should be treated equally and should educate themselves. Often, at the Capitol and Supreme Court, Mrs. Madison was seen leading a line of other women to listen to the political discussions. She held special parties just for women. When a restaurant refused to serve women, the first lady sent word that she would be coming there for lunch. The restaurant changed its policy. One American girl wrote to Dolley Madison that she was the "representative of our sex in every female virtue."

In 1817, Madison's presidency was over and Dolley retired with him to Montpelier, their home in Virginia. She missed Washington, and many in Washington missed her. Other first ladies were not as public or as popular. Elizabeth Monroe, the wife of the next president, did not continue Dolley Madison's custom of visiting the wives of important politicians. Louisa Adams,

Montpelier, the Madison house near Charlottesville, Virginia, was built around 1760 by James Madison's father.

the wife of the sixth president, was born in England and educated in France, and felt uncomfortable in public. She spent much time alone in her White House bedroom. After James Madison died in 1836, however, Dolley Madison came back to Washington.

Although she had no official role, Dolley was treated by many presidents as a "Queen Mother," and she was always invited to White House parties and family dinners. When President Van Buren came into office, he had no female relative who could be first lady. So Dolley introduced Van Buren's son to her cousin Angelica Singleton. After they married, Angelica became first lady. When Julia Gardiner, President John Tyler's bride, came to the White House, she turned to Dolley Madison for advice on how to be a good first lady. Although Sarah Polk, the wife of the eleventh president, did not play card games or dance like Dolley Madison, they became close friends. But Dolley also stayed friends with the Catholic nuns in Washington and still took an interest in the orphanage for girls.

Dolley Madison lived to be a very old lady. When citizens came to Washington, they often visited her, just to hear her tell stories about George Washington and Thomas Jefferson. The government even gave her a special seat of honor with congressmen, and chose her to send the second telegraph code message after its inventor Samuel Morse sent the first one. At the age of 81, Dolley Madison died in 1849, just 12 years before the Civil War began. All of Washington mourned her passing.

The twelfth president of the United States, Zachary

Tennessean Sarah Childress Polk (1803-1891), more outspoken and judgmental than her husband, President James K. Polk (1795-1849), believed it her religious duty to ban music, dancing, and alcohol from the White House, where she employed many slaves.

Taylor, and his first lady, Margaret Smith, attended Dolley's funeral. The president stated that Dolley Madison "will never be forgotten, because she was truly our first lady for a half-century." For years to come, Dolley Madison was the woman all others held up as the best example of first lady.

Mary Todd Lincoln with sons William (or Willie), left, and Thomas (or Tad) in 1860. Sadly, she would outlive both of them.

2

Mary Lincoln

*F*or some Americans who lived in the southern states in the first half of the nineteenth century (the period from 1800 to about 1860), slavery was a part of life. Yet for many of them, particularly women, the idea of owning another human being to work for them was wrong. One such woman, from a wealthy, famous, and important Kentucky family, used her role as first lady to act against the institution of slavery. She was married to Abraham Lincoln, one of the most famous and loved presidents. Mary Todd Lincoln, a woman of strong feelings, talked about what she believed in.

Mary was born in Lexington, Kentucky, on December 13, 1818. Her mother died when she was young, and her father, Robert Todd, influenced her greatly. Mr. Todd owned African-Americans as slaves,

Robert Todd (1791-1849) introduced his daughter, Mary, to politics, and sparked an interest in her that would help to draw her to her future husband.

but as an abolitionist who wanted the United States to ultimately be rid of slavery, Mr. Todd planned to some-day give these slaves their freedom.

Elizabeth Parker, Mary's grandmother, was an abolitionist who helped slaves escape to freedom on the Underground Railroad. Not really a railroad, this method of escape was used by fleeing slaves. They were taken from the house of one abolitionist to the house of another until they reached the North where slavery was illegal. Having crossed the Mason-Dixon line, the border between the North and South, the slave was free unless captured later by a bounty hunter.

Grandmother Parker's back fence had a mark on it that was a sign to escaped slaves that they could stop there for food and shelter as they fled North. As a little girl, Mary came to love her African-American friends and hated the idea of slavery. From her bedroom window, she could see the town square where the auctioneers sold slaves.

Mr. Todd was also interested in politics, and one of his best friends was Henry Clay, the leading politician of the Whig party, which believed in eventual abolition. As a young girl, Mary loved to listen to the political conversations between her father and Mr. Clay. She even joked to Mr. Clay that if he ever became president she would live with him in the White House.

At that time, most girls were not allowed to express their interest in politics, but Mary did. When William Henry Harrison won the election for president in 1840, Mary wrote to a friend, "This fall I became quite a politician, rather an unladylike profession, yet at such a crisis, whose heart could remain untouched while the energies of all were called into question?"

Mary went to an excellent school where boys were also students. There she learned to speak perfect French; she studied astronomy and memorized Shakespeare and other classics. Like Julia Tyler, the first lady then in the White House, Mary also loved to dance the waltz. When she visited her older sister in the town of Springfield, Illinois, a tall lawyer approached her at a party and said, "Miss Todd, I want to dance with you in the worst way." After he stepped on her toes as they waltzed, Mary joked, "And he certainly did." His name was Abraham Lincoln.

Lincoln was poor, but Mary saw much hope for a successful career in him. She told a friend, "I would rather marry a good man—a man of mind—with a hope and bright prospects ahead for position, fame, and power than to marry all the houses of gold in the world." She and Abraham married in 1842. The Lincolns had four sons: Robert, Edward (who died as a baby), Willie, and Thomas, who was also called Tad.

Mrs. Lincoln loved her home in Springfield and spent much money decorating it. She also helped start the town's first public library. However, Mary was most interested in politics. When Lincoln ran for Congress in 1846, a friend thought that Mary had "a more restless ambition" than Abraham did.

After the election, Mary visited the White House for the first time. After she left Washington, however, her husband wrote to her that some store owners contacted him because she bought things on credit: she promised

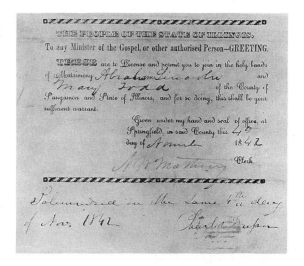

The marriage license of Abraham Lincoln and Mary Todd, dated November 4, 1842

to pay for something later that she was allowed to take home at that time. "I hesitated to pay them," Abraham wrote to Mary, "because my recollection is that you told me when you went away, there was nothing left unpaid." Not paying attention to how much she spent on things, not being able to save her money, and not paying her bills were bad habits that would always cause Mary Lincoln trouble.

When Abraham Lincoln ran for president in 1860 as a Republican, Mary was determined that he would win. She did all she could to help. She chose the pictures of him that were used on posters and other campaign items. She watched him debate Stephen Douglas, his Democratic opponent. She also began writing letters to important people in the Republican party, getting advice

With her strong interest in politics, Mary worked hard to advance her husband's career, contributing to the design of his campaign posters among other activities.

and information from them that she then gave to Lincoln. When he won the election, a newspaper said that America should be happy it had a new president who "does not reject, even in important matters, the advice and counsel of his wife."

Lincoln faced the biggest problem any president ever had. For many reasons, one of which was the fact that the southern states did not want to abolish slavery, the South decided to form its own separate government. In 1861, the "slave" states formed an alliance called the Confederate States of America, and broke away from the United States, or "the Union." The United States kept weapons at Fort Sumter, in the southern state of South Carolina. Union troops held the fort. When Confederate soldiers attacked the fort, the Civil War began.

The Civil War was the most painful time in American history because many families had relatives in both the Confederacy and the Union. Thus, relatives fought against one another in battles and sometimes killed each other. No one was more aware of this than Mrs. Lincoln, the new first lady. Married to the Union president, she was loyal to the North. But most of her family supported the Confederacy, and she had many male relatives who fought for the South. Many Northerners hated Mary because they thought she was a spy for the South, but many Southerners also hated her because she was loyal to the North.

The first lady faced other problems as well. She redecorated and bought new china for the White House at a time when the government had a war to fight and needed funding. Northerners greatly criticized her for buying these unnecessary items during wartime. On the other hand, when she decided not to spend money on band concerts for the public, others criticized her for not realizing that people needed to keep their spirits up. In addition, Mary Lincoln felt that part of her role as first lady was to look as good as she could because she had to represent her country. Yet once again, many criticized her because they thought her clothing was a waste of money and unimportant during a war. Finally, she told a friend, "I intend to wear what I please."

Many first ladies are criticized only for their actions or their style. But no matter what Mary Lincoln did, people criticized her. This was especially true of the newspapers of the time. These papers mentioned Mary more than any first lady since Dolley Madison. But instead of praising her as they had Dolley, the newspapers usually criticized Mary. One new tradition was set, however. Now, newspapers used the expression "first lady" all the time to describe the president's wife.

Mrs. Lincoln knew the men of the cabinet very well. She did not trust them all, especially William Seward, the secretary of state, and Salmon Chase, the secretary of the treasury. She thought that Seward was not strong enough on abolition, and that Chase was interested only in his own career. She shared her viewpoints with her husband, but he allowed the two men to stay in the cabinet. So, Mrs. Lincoln talked to other politicians around the country and tried to get them to tell the president to get rid of Seward and Chase.

At other times, the president did listen to his wife's ideas. He let her help many citizens get jobs in the

Former slave Elizabeth (Lizzie) Keckley (1824-1907) not only created Mary Lincoln's expensive dresses, she also strengthened the first lady's abolitionist views and helped her with the rambunctious Lincoln sons.

government. When he trusted people who were not always honest, Mary tried to warn him about them. As she said, "My husband placed great confidence in my knowledge of human nature." Mary was close friends with Senator Charles Sumner, a famous abolitionist. She brought the senator to the president for many conversations about abolition, and Abraham came to understand the human suffering of slavery even better.

Abolition remained important to Mrs. Lincoln. When she first came to the White House, she hired an African-American woman named Lizzie Keckley to work as her dressmaker. Lizzie was a former slave, and told Mary many stories of her years before freedom. She said, "I know what freedom is, because I know what slavery was." This strengthened Mary's belief that all slaves must be free.

Lizzie became Mary's best friend. Some people made fun of this friendship: A newspaper cartoonist drew a hateful cartoon that appeared in the newspaper and made fun of Mrs. Lincoln. Once when Mary and Lizzie went to a hotel, the manager refused to allow Lizzie to sleep in a room; she was sent to the attic. Mary decided that she must be with her friend, and so she slept in the attic too. Mary did not care what other people said about her friendship. She valued it.

First ladies before Mary Lincoln had worked on different projects or helped people. Abigail Fillmore, the wife of the thirteenth president, began the first White House library. Jane Pierce helped to get an abolitionist out of prison. Harriet Lane, James Buchanan's niece and first lady, helped a tribe of Native Americans. Julia Tyler helped to convince politicians to make Texas a state. Sarah Polk was her husband's secretary during the Mexican War.

Mary Lincoln decided that helping African-Americans would be part of her role. With Lizzie, she helped to form a Washington organization called The Contraband Relief Association. This organization helped former slaves get jobs, homes, and an education. Mrs. Lincoln gave money to the group and also asked many of her rich friends to contribute funds.

As first lady she also got jobs for African-Americans who asked for her help. She became the first first lady to

The Lincoln family in 1861, from left to right: Mary, Willie, Robert, Tad, and Abraham

welcome African-Americans to the White House as guests. She even let a Sunday school group have its picnic on the lawn and ordered the staff to "have everything done in the grand style" for them.

As time went on, many abolitionists heard about Mary Lincoln's interest. Jane Swisshelm, a famous abolitionist, came to visit Mary and had many talks with her about freeing the slaves. Mrs. Swisshelm said that Mary was "more radically opposed to slavery" than the president and "urged him to a matter of Emancipation as a matter of right, long before he saw it as a matter of necessity." This meant that Mary wanted slaves freed as soon as possible even though her husband wanted to wait until the time was politically right.

When Abraham Lincoln signed the Emancipation

Proclamation on New Year's Day in 1863, he freed the slaves. This was as much an accomplishment for Mary as it was for him. She wrote to a friend about the "emancipation from the great evil that has been so long allowed to curse the land. The decree had gone forth that all men are free. It is a rich and precious legacy."

Meanwhile, the Civil War was still going on. Thousands of young soldiers were being killed and wounded. Mrs. Lincoln worked as a nurse in the hospitals. She put medicine on wounds and brought the soldiers food and drink, and citrus fruits that provided vitamins. She brought them fresh baked breads and bouquets of flowers from the White House. Many soldiers loved her, and one group even named its camp "Camp Mary Lincoln." The first lady even took an interest in what kind of horses the Union soldiers were using. Mrs. Lincoln was also one of the first people to tell her husband to get a new leader of the Union Army because George McClellan was too slow in planning how the troops should fight. Lincoln chose Ulysses S. Grant to be the new general. When Mary and Abraham came to visit General Grant's headquarters, they met his wife, Julia Dent.

In 1864, Northerners elected Abraham Lincoln for another four years as president. Mary's years as first lady had been very hard. During those years, her little son Willie had died, but many people didn't think she had a right to be sad since so many other mothers had sons who were dying in the war. However, Willie's death upset Mary greatly. Mrs. Lincoln's feelings often changed unexpectedly, and sometimes people, not understanding her mood swings, were unable to get along with her.

In April 1865, General Robert E. Lee, the leader of the Confederate army, finally signed a peace treaty with General Grant. Now the war was over and the South rejoined the Union. A few days later, the Lincolns went to the theater to see a play. A man who had supported the Confederacy shot and killed the president. This act changed Mrs. Lincoln's life forever.

When she left the White House with Lizzie and her sons, Tad and Robert, Mary moved to Chicago. When she was first lady, she had bought many beautiful clothes on credit. Now she was unable to pay her bills. When she asked Congress for money, they gave her some, but not enough. Then Mrs. Lincoln left America for a few years to live in different countries, including Scotland, France, Germany, and Italy, because living abroad did not cost as much as living in the United States.

Depressed, Mrs. Lincoln could not always think clearly and was frightened. She believed that people were plotting against her. However, at this time, there were no psychiatrists to whom she could talk about her worries. So, she had to go to a special hospital for a few months. When Mrs. Lincoln returned from living abroad, she went to live with her sister.

In 1869, Ulysses S. Grant, the former general of the Union army in the Civil War was elected president. Mrs. Grant had great influence over her husband and even helped choose men for his cabinet. Like Mary Todd Lincoln, Mrs. Grant's family had also been from the South and owned slaves, and Julia Dent Grant redecorated the White House and dressed in stylish clothes as Mary Lincoln had, but newspapers liked her. This shows how ideas about first ladies can change in different times. When Mrs. Grant was first lady, the country was not fighting a civil war.

However, the first lady who had the most influence on Mary Lincoln's life was Lucretia Garfield. Mrs. Garfield was also very interested in politics. After her husband was elected as the twentieth president of the United States, Mrs. Garfield hoped to bring back furniture and paintings to the White House that had been used there before.

Like Abraham Lincoln, Mrs. Garfield's husband, James, was killed by an assassin's bullet. Congress decided to give her a certain amount of money each year. Many people realized that giving the same to the wives of other presidents who were dead was only fair. So, Congress finally gave Mary the money she needed. Only a few months after she got the money, however, Mary Lincoln died.

People did not always like the things Mary Todd Lincoln said or did, especially with regard to slavery and abolition. However, if Mrs. Lincoln felt that she was doing what was right, she acted.

Sadly, Mrs. Lincoln had a life full of troubles. She knew that money or fame did not ensure a happy life. As Mary Lincoln said, "You must enjoy life whenever you can. I know full well by experience that power and high position do not ensure a bed of roses."

President William H. Taft thought so much of his wife's political skills that he once addressed a note to Nellie: "Memorandum for Mrs. Taft—the real President from the nominal President."

3

Nellie Taft

As the twentieth century began, Americans encoun-
tered some exciting times. Telephones appeared in
most homes. Automobiles would soon make distances
seem shorter. Radio would eventually provide not only
news but entertainment. Instead of listening to record-
ed music on long, tube-like cylinders, people could now
use the flat, round "record." In the sky, the Wright
brothers were working on their new project, the airplane. In the first decade of the 1900s, a modern first
lady, who enjoyed many of the new inventions as much
as she enjoyed her role, came to the White House.
Helen Herron Taft, nicknamed Nellie, had always wanted to be first lady.

Born on June 2, 1861, Nellie was raised in
Cincinnati, Ohio. For many years, Americans thought

of Cincinnati as the Far West, the way we now think of California. Settled in the 1700s, the city had many good schools. Nellie Herron attended one of these, run by a Miss Nourse.

As a young girl, Nellie excelled at music and said it inspired her dreams. She was also good at many subjects that would not lead to a career for women at that time. She was especially interested in politics and economics.

When she was 16, her father let her visit the White House where his friend, Rutherford Hayes, lived as nineteenth president of the United States. Nellie went to many events with Lucy Hayes, the first lady. Later, Mrs. Taft said that "nothing in my life reaches the climax of human bliss I felt when, as a girl of 16, I was entertained at the White House." As the most exciting moment of her young life, the event made her ambitious. She wanted to live in the White House one day.

As a young woman, Nellie lived in what was called the Victorian Age, named after England's famous Queen Victoria. Miss Herron did not like many rules that people lived by in the Victorian Age because she thought that society did not allow women to do as much as men.

After she finished school, Nellie became a teacher. She wanted to work and earn her own money so her father would not have to support her. She also gathered around her a group of other young people who discussed politics and economics. A lawyer, William Howard Taft, was part of that group. Nellie called him Will. When they went on dates, Nellie insisted on paying half the cost of the rented horse and buggy.

Will was impressed by Nellie and wrote a relative that "she wanted to do something in life and not be a burden. Her eagerness for knowledge of all kinds puts me to shame. Her capacity for work is just wonderful." He fell in love with Nellie and begged, "Do say that you will try and love me. Oh, how I will work and strive to be better and do better, and how I will labor for our joint advancement if you will only let me."

Nellie married Will in 1886. After she visited Washington again, Will joked that if they were ever to work in politics, she would become secretary of the treasury.

Back in Cincinnati, Nellie helped create an orchestra symphony. In doing so, she worked with many people of the Jewish faith and became good friends with them. Unlike many other people at the time, Mrs. Taft had no prejudices against people of different races and religions.

The Tafts had three children, Robert, Helen, and Charles, and Nellie made sure they were given good educations. Will Taft worked as a judge and then as a

Nellie Taft in the 1890s with two of her children, Helen (left) and Robert

The daughter of an Ohio banker, Ida Saxton McKinley (1844-1907) was one of the wealthiest first ladies. However, she suffered from uncontrollable epilepsy, and the powerful drugs she took affected her appearance.

law professor in Ohio. But more than anything, Mrs. Taft wanted to live in Washington and get her husband into politics. Her wish was soon granted.

At the time, the first lady was Ida McKinley. Mrs. McKinley was also from Ohio and she gave her husband opinions on how America should run the Philippines. After winning the Spanish-American War, America had obtained the Philippine Islands from Spain. President McKinley decided to put William Howard Taft in charge of the Philippines.

Will and Nellie went to California on the west coast

of America and sailed across the Pacific Ocean to move into their new home in the Philippines. When they stopped in Hawaii, Nellie even tried surfing.

Living in Manila, the capital of the Philippines, was different from living in Ohio. Nellie danced Filipino dances and even dressed in the native costume with high sleeves, called butterfly sleeves. At her parties for visiting Americans she always invited native Filipinos.

Many people were surprised when Nellie decided to take a horseback journey into the mountains with men and visit the natives in the areas called the Luzon. She was the first white woman ever to explore the Luzon. Nellie also started a special program to help the poor people of the Philippines who needed milk to keep their babies alive. She called this campaign "Drop of Milk." When the babies and children grew up healthy, they often came to see Mrs. Taft. Although the Taft family was Protestant, Mrs. Taft attended some of the Filipino Roman Catholic church services. Later, she sent her daughter to a Catholic school.

When President McKinley was shot, the vice-president, Theodore Roosevelt became the twenty-sixth president. He appointed Taft to his cabinet as the secretary of war, and the Tafts moved to Washington. Nellie said that "this was much more pleasing to me because it was in line with the kind of work I wanted my husband to do." She also made exciting trips around the world with Will, exploring new cultures in Russia, Japan, Panama, Cuba, Germany, and Italy.

However, Will's dream was to someday be appointed to the Supreme Court as chief justice, in charge of the judicial branch of government. One night, President Roosevelt was joking to the Tafts that he had had a dream. In his dream Roosevelt saw a line above Mr. Taft's head, but he couldn't read what it said. "Make it the chief justiceship," said Will. "Make it the presidency!" said Nellie.

Even though Will was good friends with President Roosevelt, Nellie did not become close to him or to his first lady, Edith Carow Roosevelt.

Mrs. Roosevelt was more interested in staying out of public and keeping her life as private as she could. She worked on creating a presidential image for the White House when it had to be renovated, with the walls, floors, and rooms repaired and remodeled. Mrs. Taft, of course, was interested in politics and public events, and never minded being photographed or quoted.

Nellie also did not believe Mr. Roosevelt when he said that he did not want to be president after the 1908 election. She went to the White House to meet Roosevelt privately. They argued because Nellie thought he was not giving enough support to Taft for president. This action was unlike anything most politicians' wives would do at the time.

During the presidential campaign, many people thought that Mrs. Taft wanted to live in the White House more than her husband did. She listened to his speeches and advised him not to talk about President Roosevelt too much. She went with him to rallies. She made sure that her husband did not do things that the newspapers would criticize.

Will won the presidency, and Nellie started getting

ready for her new role. As manager of the White House, she made all the ushers get new blue uniforms and hired a new housekeeper. Even though Will wanted certain men in his cabinet, Nellie, in her role as political advisor, suggested other men that she thought were more suitable. About many of the political problems facing him, Taft admitted that he felt "like a fish out of water" but that "as my wife is the politician she will be able to meet all these issues."

Nellie started a new tradition on Inauguration Day, March 4, 1909. After Will was sworn in as president, the outgoing president, Theodore Roosevelt, decided not to ride back to the White House in the presidential carriage, as had always been done. Mrs. Taft said, "I see no reason why the President's wife may not now come into some rights on that day." So, Nellie Taft, as the new first lady, rode back to the White House with her new president. She said it was her proudest moment. "I had secret elation in doing something no woman had ever done." Every first lady since that time has now done so.

One of the most daring things that Nellie did was to make a deal with a car company. She asked them to provide the Taft family with free cars, and agreed to let them advertise that their cars were used at the White House. Nellie Taft was a very different kind of first lady. Other first ladies in the Victorian Age had helped women. Caroline Harrison, wife of the twenty-third president, worked with a group that wanted a medical school that would admit women. Frances Cleveland held special receptions on Saturday afternoons so young women who worked all week could come talk to her on their day off.

However, no first lady had ever told reporters that she wanted women to be given the right to vote. Nellie Taft was the first to do so. She also wanted all women to have the chance to get college educations. Nellie maintained that "no fundamental superiority or inferiority" existed between men and women. "The only superiority lies in the way in which the responsibilities of life are discharged." Mrs. Taft helped many citizens. When a woman from the South wanted to start a kindergarten for African-American children, Nellie invited her to come to the White House for a meeting. She helped other women get jobs in government.

At this time in American history, millions of Europeans were coming to live in America. Mrs. Taft was always trying to help these immigrants. For instance, she helped an immigrant boy who was refused admittance to the United States because he had a speech problem. With Mrs. Taft's help he was allowed into America. When an Italian girl was badly injured in an accident in a Massachusetts factory, Mrs. Taft went to Congress and listened to her story. The newspapers wrote about the first lady being there, and this event helped to start an investigation about working conditions in factories.

What became her most famous project, however, still delights millions of visitors who come to Washington in the springtime. Mrs. Taft wanted to establish a park near an artificial lake called the Tidal Basin. She made arrangements with the city of Tokyo in Japan to have thousands of Japanese cherry trees donated to America for her park. Nellie planted the first tree, and she also started free band concerts there for the public. Every spring, the famous Washington cherry trees still send forth their white and pink blossoms.

Mrs. Taft also stayed interested in the president's work. Many times she surprised people by coming to his meetings where important politicians gathered. Sometimes, when she saw her husband talking to a politician at a party, she joined the conversation.

Many people noticed that Mrs. Taft worked hard. As time went on, however, she worked too hard. She became nervous and tired. One day, while taking a boat cruise, she suffered a paralytic stroke. Because of this, one side of her body became paralyzed. She could not even talk.

The president and his children were very worried. Will decided not to tell Nellie about his work because it might upset her. But little by little, she grew stronger. Mr. Taft even taught her to speak again.

In two years, Mrs. Taft was once more ready to attend public events. The greatest event of her White House years was a huge lawn party celebrating her and Will's twenty-fifth wedding anniversary, called a silver anniversary. People from all across the country sent the Tafts silver gifts. Nellie invited all the important Jewish rabbis, Protestant ministers, and Catholic priests to be among the many thousands of guests.

In 1912, Will had to decide whether to run for president again. Nellie wanted him to, but she was worried that former President Roosevelt would challenge him. Will didn't think this would happen, but Nellie was proven right.

Because the Republican party nominated Taft, Roosevelt decided to form his own new party, the Progressives. The Democrats nominated Woodrow Wilson. Both Taft and Roosevelt lost to Wilson.

After losing the election, the Tafts moved to Connecticut, where Mr. Taft taught at Yale University. He still had his dream of becoming chief justice of the

A family portrait taken at the White House on June 18, 1911, to celebrate the Tafts' twenty-fifth wedding anniversary. Standing, from left, are: Robert, the Tafts' son; Maria Herron, Nellie's sister; Horace, the president's brother; Helen, the Tafts' daughter; Henry, the president's brother; and Charles, the Tafts' younger son. Seated, from left, are: Mrs. Charles Anderson, Nellie's sister; Nellie; the president; Delia Torrey, the president's aunt; and Mrs. Henry Taft.

Supreme Court. When Warren Harding became president in 1921, he granted Will his wish. The Tafts returned to Washington.

During the next few years, Mrs. Taft was often at the White House visiting other first ladies with whom she became friends: Florence Harding, Grace Coolidge, and Lou Hoover. Will died in 1930, but Nellie stayed in Washington. She often made trips to Europe on her own, and every spring she went down to South Carolina to see the beautiful gardens in bloom. In Washington, she liked going to lectures and music concerts instead of parties.

In 1940, Eleanor Roosevelt, wife of the thirty-second president, invited Nellie Taft to the White House. This was her last visit to the place she had loved since childhood. She died in 1943.

Nellie Taft was a bold woman who loved politics. She lived in a day when women were not elected to political office, so she worked in this area as best she could, through her husband. As she said, "I had always had the satisfaction of knowing almost as much as he about the politics and intricacies of any situation. I think any woman can discuss with her husband topics of national interest. I became familiar with more than politics. It involved real statesmanship."

On November 2, 1920, Warren G. Harding stands with his wife, Florence, outside a voting booth, where she would become the first woman whose vote helped to elect her husband president.

4

Florence Harding

*I*n 1920, the U.S. Constitution was amended to grant American women the right to vote. After many years, organizations of women finally convinced Congress to change the Constitution, the document that states the rights of American citizens, by adding the Nineteenth Amendment. That same year, Florence Harding became the first woman in history to vote for her husband to become president. When Warren Harding won the election, Florence was not afraid to tell people how much she had helped.

Florence Mabel Kling was born on August 15, 1860, in the small town of Marion, Ohio. She could remember watching, as a little girl, Union soldiers marching home from the Civil War in their blue uniforms.

Florence's father owned many businesses. He had a hardware store but also went into banking and buying land, which he then rented to farmers. Mr. Kling had wanted his first child to be a son, but when a daughter was born instead, he decided to teach her the same things about business that he would have taught a son. Florence said that her father also taught her that "to be in

The child from Florence Harding's first marriage, Marshall De Wolfe, pictured here at age ten, would later give her two grandchildren.

the middle of the road was not all there was to a journey, but that I must look to the right, and to the left and observe and look and listen if I would count myself alive." She learned to carefully observe every situation in life.

Florence was excellent in mathematics and learned accounting and how to make money investments. In school, she learned how to play the piano and practiced three hours a day. Florence also loved sports. In the winter, she was able to take many other children on her bobsled and glide down snowy hills without anyone falling off. In the summer, she rode her horse and when he started to buck, she took control.

Florence would sometimes go rollerskating with a neighbor, Henry De Wolfe. Both Florence's and Henry's parents thought they were too young to get married. They were in love, however, and eloped in 1880. They had a son, Marshall.

Henry and Florence's marriage ended in divorce. This experience taught Florence how to take care of herself. She let her parents help with her son, Marshall, and she made money for herself by becoming a piano teacher. One of her students was a girl named Charity Harding. Florence met Charity's brother, Warren, and the two fell in love. Once again, Florence's father did not think she should get married. This time, however, Florence was 31 years old, and accustomed to making her own decisions. She and Warren Harding got married in a new house that he was building.

Warren Harding owned a newspaper in town called *The Marion Star*. As the editor, he decided what stories would be in the newspaper, but he did not pay much attention to the business side of publishing. Florence took over the management of the paper. She made sure that customers got their newspapers and that they paid on time. Florence Harding is one of only a few first ladies who worked after she got married. At first she went down to the *Star* office, "intending to help out for a few days." However, she stayed for 14 years.

Mrs. Harding also thought that having newspaper boys deliver the papers every morning would be a good idea. Not only did this idea help make more money for *The Marion Star*, it also gave jobs to the little boys in town and taught them important lessons about how to help themselves. When many of the newsboys grew up, they had good jobs and stayed close to Mrs. Harding.

Mrs. Harding's family life differed from most of the other first ladies. She and Mr. Harding did not have any children together, although Marshall came and lived with them part of the time. Florence and Warren loved each other, but they put emphasis on their work together as business partners. The Hardings also had many close friends, and they took vacations and celebrated

59

holidays with them. One of their friends, Harry Daugherty, worked in Ohio politics. Harry thought that Warren would be effective in politics. With Florence's help, Warren was elected a state senator and then the lieutenant governor, the most important person in Ohio politics after the governor. In 1914, the state of Ohio elected Warren Harding to the United States Senate, and he and Florence moved to Washington, D.C.

Florence loved being the wife of a senator in Washington and enjoyed being part of her husband's work in politics. At the time, Woodrow Wilson was president, and America had entered World War I to assist England, France, and Italy in their war with Germany. Mrs. Harding often went to the train station with her best friend, Evalyn McLean, to distribute food and drinks to the soldiers who were traveling to the ships that would sail to Europe.

All across the country, women gave their time to help the cause. Older first ladies did their part too. Lucretia Garfield, who had been first lady in 1881, worked in California for the Red Cross. Edith Roosevelt knitted socks and sweaters for the soldiers. Frances Cleveland, who was married in the White House in 1886, gave speeches asking people to help any way they could.

When the war was over, President Wilson wanted to start the League of Nations. This organization of different countries would form an international army to stop one country from invading another. Suddenly President Wilson had a stroke, which left him partially paralyzed. His first wife, Ellen Axson Wilson, had died in the White House in 1914. In 1915, he married Edith

Bolling Wilson. Now, because he was sick, his second wife helped him by controlling the great amount of work he had to do as president. She did not want anyone to know how weak he was, so she did not let many important politicians see him. This caused people to exaggerate and accuse Edith of being the first woman president.

The Wilsons were Democrats, and the Hardings were Republicans. Warren and Florence Harding did not think the League of Nations was a good idea. They thought that the organization might force the United States to fight in future wars that the country did not

Edith Bolling Wilson (1872-1961) proudly traced her ancestry to Pocahontas, the Indian woman who in the early 1600s befriended the colonists in Jamestown, Virginia. She was, however, highly intolerant of other American minorities, including blacks, Jews, and Catholics. And although she was President Wilson's closest advisor, Edith also despised suffragettes—people who wanted to allow women to vote.

61

Florence Harding's deep friendship with Evalyn McLean, pictured here between the Hardings, covered everything from fashion, to gardening, to politics.

believe in. Because of this belief, the Hardings' friend, Harry Daugherty, asked Warren to run for president and helped him to become the Republican candidate.

Florence worked hard to get Warren elected. Since this was the first time women were allowed to vote for a president, she frequently talked about how women must learn about their country and about politics. Whenever groups of women came to see Harding, she would always welcome them and explain why they should vote for him. In the past, many candidates' wives were too shy to allow photographs of themselves in newspapers, but not Florence. She was proud of her work. And Warren told everyone that "anything I've ever gotten I owe to Mrs. Harding."

As first lady, Florence was always busy. In private, she helped the president with many of his political ideas and made suggestions on what he should say in his speeches. She was always careful that Warren never let people think he liked the idea of a League of Nations. However, Florence Harding did not make people angry as Edith Wilson had. They were both powerful in politics, but in different ways. Florence did not try to keep things from Warren as Edith had done with Woodrow. Americans liked the fact that Florence told the truth about how much she helped the president.

The Hardings were in the White House during the Jazz Age, so named because the most popular music was the new sound of jazz. Florence had a jazz band play at the White House and also owned a radio, which was a new item in many American homes at the time. She liked the new dances, which her friend Evalyn often did, and she wore many of the new styles for women. Even a color, "Harding Blue," was named for her. Florence Harding also liked taking rides in her "machine," the popular name for automobiles at the time.

Sometimes, Grace Coolidge, the vice-president's wife (also called the second lady) helped Florence entertain guests. Mrs. Coolidge was youthful and warm, with a good sense of humor. Many people liked her personality. She had been a teacher of the deaf and this would become her special project when she became first lady.

Florence Harding was especially interested in the children of the United States. Whenever she went somewhere, she always wanted to ask children about themselves. She liked the idea of Girl Scouts and Campfire Girls because, she said, "There is no reason girls should not be permitted to enjoy physical exercise." She ordered that the Easter egg roll, which had been stopped during

World War I, be held once again for children. Mrs. Harding used her power to help immigrant children and those in reform schools who needed special attention from the government to solve their problems.

Florence thought that taking care of the thousands of disabled veterans, American soldiers who had come back wounded in World War I, was important. So she often visited the hospitals where they were being cared for, and gave special garden parties for them. When Mrs. Harding got letters from their families asking for help in getting what was promised to the soldiers, she told important politicians to find out what the problem was and see if it could be solved. She called the veterans "my boys."

Friendship was an important part of Florence's life. When she needed to rest from all the work she did, her friend Evalyn McLean would take her to movies and

Always an active woman herself, Florence strongly supported the Girl Scouts, the recreational and service organization founded in 1912.

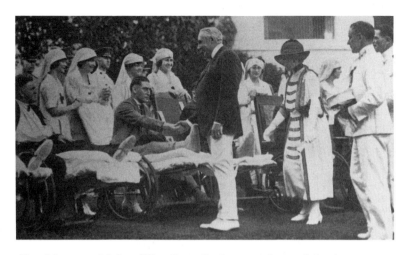

President and Mrs. Harding (in her trademark hat) greet wounded veterans of World War I. Mrs. Harding regularly visited army hospitals, where she passed out gifts and wrote letters for blind and injured soldiers.

plays or invite Florence to stay at her beautiful mansion, which was called Friendship.

In September 1922, Mrs. Harding became very sick. She almost died, but Florence had a strong mind and wanted to live. Many people prayed for Mrs. Harding to get well, especially the children of America who wrote to her and sent flowers to the White House. Little by little, Florence recovered.

Warren and Florence Harding had many friends whom they thought were honest, and they gave these friends important jobs in politics. They did not know that some of these friends lied and cheated. One friend, Charlie Forbes, was supposed to take care of the veterans. When the Hardings found out that he was embezzling money, they were deeply hurt. As a cabinet member, Albert Fall let oil companies take oil that was supposed to be for the use of the government at different properties in America, such as the Teapot Dome in Wyoming. Also, the Hardings' old friend Harry Daugherty had an assistant who was selling liquor at a time when it was illegal. Newspapers and citizens alike labeled these events "scandals." However, Warren and Florence did no wrong. They only trusted too much.

In 1923, the president wanted to explain his policies better to the people. He and Florence took a train trip across the United States and a boat trip to Alaska so he could speak to crowds. On this trip, the president suddenly died while Florence was reading to him. Lou Hoover, the wife of a cabinet member, and other friends helped as Florence made the train trip back to Washington with the dead president. He was buried in their hometown of Marion, Ohio. Then Florence returned to Washington and helped put his government papers in order. Afterward, she moved back to Marion, where she died on November 22, 1924.

Even though she had many hard times, Florence Harding always put her energy into the good things she had in her life. Instead of becoming sad for long periods of time, she saw difficulties as a challenge to improve herself and as a chance to learn something new. One lesson of her life was the importance of friendship. Just because a few friends did illegal things, Florence did not stop being close to those friends who were honest and true. She always tried to understand what made other people do the things they did. As she said, "after all, about the best part there is in all of us is the real human part."

5
Eleanor Roosevelt

*N*ever before had America suffered as badly from the economic problems known as a depression as it did in the early 1930s. Many people were out of work. Neighbors and government had to help needy families. The people of the Great Depression also needed hope to keep going until jobs and money came their way again. The one woman who seemed to give the most hope was also the first lady. She was first lady longer than any other before or since. From 1933 to 1945, Eleanor Roosevelt worked as the most active first lady in American history. After that, she became what President Harry Truman called "first lady of the World."

Being so important was not the kind of life most people would have imagined for Eleanor when she was a young girl. She was born on October 11, 1884, in New York City.

No first lady before or since Eleanor Roosevelt worked as long and as tirelessly as she to improve the welfare of ordinary Americans. Here she holds her baby, Anna Eleanor.

The Roosevelts were wealthy and famous in New York, but they had their share of problems. Eleanor's mother, Anna Hall, was beautiful. Eleanor was not, and sometimes Anna called her "Granny." This hurt the girl's feelings. Eleanor idolized her father, but he had a problem with alcohol.

Both of Eleanor's parents died when she was young. She was sent to live with her stern Grandmother Hall at her mansion on the Hudson River. In the summers and during holidays, Eleanor lived with her Uncle Theodore and his wife, Edith. The Roosevelts had five children, including the oldest, Alice, who was Theodore's daughter by his first wife. Alice was always speaking her mind, leading the children, and getting attention. Eleanor was shy and felt insecure. However, Edith Roosevelt said of Eleanor that "the ugly duckling may turn out to be a swan" someday.

Eleanor's grandmother sent her to the Allenswood School in England taught by Madame Souvestre. There she began to learn about politics, which was an interest of Madame Souvestre's. For the first time, she also began to make close friends.

When Miss Eleanor Roosevelt returned to America, her Uncle Theodore was president of the United States. On the train heading to her grandmother's home, she ran into her second cousin, Franklin Delano Roosevelt. As children they had played piggyback together, and as young people, they had gone to many parties together. When Eleanor visited her uncle in the White House, Franklin was also visiting Washington. Her intelligence interested him.

Miss Roosevelt began working as a volunteer with a group called the Junior League. She taught immigrant children at the Rivington Street Settlement. For the Consumers League, she went into crowded apartments to check on conditions of people who worked at home. Eleanor felt best helping others, not going to fancy parties.

Franklin liked Eleanor's serious side. On St. Patrick's Day, 1905, she finally agreed to marry him. At the wedding, Theodore Roosevelt joked "Well, there's nothing like keeping the name in the family!" Eleanor and Franklin Roosevelt had five children: Anna, James, Elliott, Franklin, Jr., and John. Mrs. Roosevelt became a wife and mother, and led a traditional life, partly because she wanted to and partly because her husband's mother, Sara, had such a strong personality and told Eleanor what to do and how to live her life. So, Eleanor did what she was told, even if she really didn't want to. The Roosevelts lived in a house connected to Sara's in New York City. They spent free time at Sara's estate, Hyde Park, where Franklin had grown up. In the summer they went with Sara to Campobello Island, just across the Canadian border.

When Franklin was appointed assistant secretary of the navy by President Woodrow Wilson, the Roosevelts moved to Washington. There Eleanor met First Lady Ellen Wilson, the first wife of the president. Mrs. Wilson wanted to help the poor families who could afford to make their homes only in alleys and slums. However, before Mrs. Wilson could accomplish her goals, she died. But Eleanor Roosevelt saw the need, too, and never forgot the poor of Washington.

In 1920, Franklin Roosevelt ran for vice-president on the Democratic ticket, with James Cox of Ohio as the presidential candidate. They lost to Harding and Coolidge. Franklin returned to being a lawyer in New York, but he still wanted a career in politics. Eleanor, however, did not enjoy campaigning. "I hate politics!" she told Franklin at that time.

However, Eleanor wanted to help her husband by being a good political wife. So, she joined groups that taught her about politics, like the League of Women Voters and the women's division of New York's Democratic party. She also joined groups that improved housing conditions for people and that taught people how to buy wisely and how to make sure that they were not cheated.

In 1921, while spending the summer on Campobello Island, Franklin helped stamp out a small fire. Then he went swimming in cold water. This change from very hot to very cold caused a blood clot to form in his body. The clot became stuck in his spinal cord. Diagnosed with polio, Franklin was unable to move his legs.

This was one of the most frightening times in Eleanor's life. Franklin's mother wanted him to quit work and live at Hyde Park. But because Eleanor knew that her husband could still be active in politics, she decided to do all she could to help him. She said that this happening "made me stand on my own two feet." She made speeches for Franklin; sometimes she went to important meetings and gathered information for him.

Eleanor told Franklin that "I'm only being active until you can be again." However, she learned that the more she tried to do, the more she was able to do. Slowly, her confidence grew. For example, because she was nervous, her voice was very high. But she had to make many speeches. Little by little, she learned to control her voice. A voice-training class helped Eleanor to speak on the radio and to lecture to many groups.

When Franklin was elected governor of the state of New York in 1928, Eleanor became even more active.

His polio prevented Franklin from getting around easily. So he sent Eleanor as his "eyes and ears" to inspect schools, prisons, hospitals, and other places that the state government ran. Then she reported back to him. She said, "I learned to look into the cooking pots on the stove and to find out if the contents corresponded to the menu. I learned to notice whether the beds were close together. I learned to watch the patients' attitudes towards the staff, and before the end of our years in Albany I had become a fairly expert reporter on state conditions."

Eleanor began to do things on her own too. She became a schoolteacher at the Todhunter School in New York City. In her class on current events, Eleanor took her students to court to listen to witnesses and to police stations to watch the procedures. In her history class, she asked students to write essays on subjects like women being active in government. She started a furniture factory called Val-Kill and also wrote stories for newspapers, magazines, and books. She traveled on her own all over the United States. For the Democratic party, she started the *Democratic News*, a newsletter that came out once a month. "Women should not be afraid to soil their hands," she said. "Those who are not afraid make the best politicians."

In 1929, when Herbert Hoover was president, America suffered an economic depression. People lost their jobs and savings, and some families lost their homes. Many Americans feared that things would never get better.

Herbert Hoover and his wife, Lou Henry Hoover,

Eleanor (seated, in black dress) took a field trip to Washington in 1929 with seniors from the Todhunter School. Standing next to Eleanor is her friend and the co-owner of the school, Marion Dickerman.

did their best to help Americans during the Great Depression. Mrs. Hoover was president of the Girl Scouts and tried to get them and other citizens to help anyone they could with charity and other forms of giving. However, these efforts were not enough to lift the country out of the Depression.

Franklin Roosevelt was elected president in 1932. Now Eleanor was first lady, but she remembered when her aunt, Edith Roosevelt, had been first lady. "For myself I was deeply troubled. As I saw it, this meant the end of any personal life of my own. I knew what traditionally should lie before me. I had watched Mrs. Theodore Roosevelt and had seen what it meant to be the wife of the president, and I cannot say I was pleased."

Because the Depression had changed so much of what Americans were used to, Mrs. Roosevelt thought that she could do things differently as first lady. So she invited women reporters to come to the White House once a week and meet with her in the Green Room. This helped the women reporters keep their jobs during the Depression and also let the country know what the first lady was doing. The reporters were called "the Green Room girls."

Mrs. Roosevelt also began to write a daily newspaper column called "My Day." In it she described her work, her activities, the people she was meeting, and her thoughts on current events. She also had a radio show on Sunday nights. (At this time, most American families listened to the radio each evening.) Now people could listen to what Mrs. Roosevelt was thinking. The first lady also had a question and answer column each month in a popular magazine. Sometimes Mrs. Roosevelt went around the country and spoke to groups about her role as first lady. She gave the money she earned to charity.

Roosevelt's plan to help Americans during the Depression was called the New Deal. The New Deal meant that the government would start and pay for many special programs to help Americans. Eleanor Roosevelt became very involved in the New Deal.

Because the president had polio, Eleanor was still his "eyes and ears." She traveled everywhere around the United States. She rode over a dam that was being built. She went into shacks in the Caribbean. She flew with the famous woman aviator, Amelia Earhart. She visited Native Americans on their reservation. She popped into restaurants. Sometimes she took buses and subways, and drove her own car. She even went down into a coal mine. Sometimes people did not know that she was coming, and one of the most popular jokes in America became, "Here comes Mrs. Roosevelt!" She appeared, quite unexpectedly, in the most unusual places!

Mrs. Roosevelt was friends with many important politicians. She invited them to meet with her at breakfast, lunch, and dinner. As she tried to help others, Eleanor would ask politicians for favors. She also asked them to tell newspapers that they supported her ideas or the president's. After reading special government documents and studying how much money was set aside for New Deal programs, Eleanor offered ideas on improvements. Never before had a first lady gotten so deeply involved in the details of government and worked so hard politically.

Eleanor Roosevelt wanted to help average Americans to help themselves. She said, "I truly believe that I understand what faces the great masses of people in the country today. I have no illusions that anyone can change the world in a short time. Yet I do believe that even a few people who want to understand, to help, and to do the right thing for the great numbers of people instead of for the few can help."

Soon she realized that by being first lady she could accomplish a great deal. She told a friend, "I am in a position where I can do the most good to help the most people." Eleanor was especially interested in getting more women involved in politics. She was close to

Eleanor visiting a nursery school for black children in Des Moines, Iowa. In the 1930s, many states had separate schools for blacks and whites, but Eleanor's work and vision for the education of children was colorblind.

women like Secretary of Labor Frances Perkins, the first woman cabinet member, and Molly Dewson who was in charge of the women's division of the Democratic party. When a goverment job opened up and Mrs. Roosevelt thought that a certain woman could do the work, she always asked the president to add the woman's name to the list of other people whom he was considering for the job.

Ever since the Civil War, when African-Americans had been freed from slavery, many people had tried to stop them from getting good jobs and educations. Mrs. Roosevelt did all she could to change this. She was not always able to change government laws, but sometimes she set an example. For instance, in the South she fought segregation, a law that meant white and black people stayed separate. Once, at a meeting in Alabama, Mrs. Roosevelt sat in the section for African-Americans. Another time, she joined a protest in a restaurant that refused to serve black people. Finally, the restaurant changed its policy and served all people. When a women's group refused to let Marian Anderson, a famous African-American, sing in their hall, the first lady resigned from the group. Then she arranged for Miss Anderson to sing at the Lincoln Memorial.

Many people did not like these radical things that the first lady was doing. These people did not want to recognize the equality of African-Americans. However, Mrs. Roosevelt said, "We must not just accept things

Eleanor chats with singer Marian Anderson, the first black to perform at the White House.

that are wrong." She always defended her belief in racial equality.

She also tried to improve the lives of the coal miners of West Virginia. Although she received no pay for the job, Mrs. Roosevelt helped direct a government project called Arthurdale. She got government money to build a new community there and to teach the people how to improve their lives.

All of this made Americans more aware of their first lady than they had ever been. Very quickly Eleanor Roosevelt became the most famous first lady of all time. People thought of her in a personal way, and many felt they could go to her for help or advice. Thousands of people wrote letters to her.

Eleanor always felt that every single person was important. "Out of my response to an individual," she said, "develops an awareness of a problem to the community, then to the country, and finally to the world."

This was a new kind of first lady for America. But not everyone liked this type of first lady. Some said that she had no business talking about politics and giving her opinion. Other people thought that was trying to do the president's job.

The president did not mind her doing and saying what she wanted. "Lady, it's a free country," he told her, "If you get me into hot water, I'll manage to save myself." When politicians said they thought she should stay home and be a hostess, he told them, "My missus goes where she wants to, talks to everybody, and does she learn something!"

After Roosevelt won a second term, Eleanor stayed

just as busy. She even wrote a book about her early life. During this time the first lady began to worry about the power of the new leader of Germany, Adolf Hitler, who seemed to want to control all of Europe. She could not understand "how people of spirit could be terrified of one man." She hated Hitler's prejudice toward people who were different from himself. Mrs. Roosevelt felt that Americans had "a responsibility in the one great country that is free to the rest of the world wherever there may be people who are not free to become free again." When Roosevelt became the only president to win a third term, Eleanor became the first first lady to speak at a national political convention. She said a third term was needed because Germany wanted to conquer more free countries, like England, which was a close ally, or friend, of America. War seemed a certainty.

Eleanor's address to the Democrats in Chicago on July 18, 1940, marked the first time that a president's wife had spoken at a national party convention.

The president decided to help England fight Germany. To help the United States get ready if it had to go to war, Eleanor worked for the Office of Civilian Defense, which taught Americans how to prepare for war. She had an office outside the White House and wore a uniform every day. Often, she walked to her job. People going to work were shocked to see her.

Germany, Italy, and Japan joined together as the Axis powers. Germany took over France and Holland, and invaded Russia. On December 7, 1941, Japan surprised America by bombing Pearl Harbor in Hawaii, where American sailors and battleships were stationed. The president decided that America must fight. Thus, World War II began for the American people.

Meanwhile, Eleanor continued to work for the Office of Civilian Defense. No first lady had ever had a job of her own, and many Americans didn't like the idea of Mrs. Roosevelt working. She left the job, but once again, because the president couldn't travel, Eleanor became his "eyes and ears."

During the war, Eleanor traveled around the world. She went to England to visit American soldiers and see how they were being trained and living. She went to Australia and Guadalcanal, where one of the most famous battles of World War II took place. She visited troops stationed in the Caribbean. She also talked with nurses and volunteers from the Red Cross to see if they were getting the help they needed.

The soldiers loved Mrs. Roosevelt, and some said that she reminded them of their mothers back home in America. Even though she always had a fear of traveling

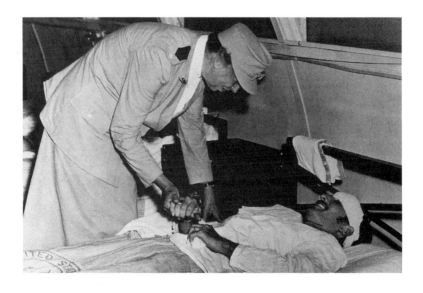

On her trip to the South Pacific in August and September of 1943, Eleanor combined morale-boosting speeches to the troops with hospital visits to wounded soldiers.

over water, Eleanor forced herself to be fearless by simply doing what had to be done. She took her typewriter on her travels and typed her daily newspaper stories in her spare time. She even had her own gas mask, just in case she was ever caught someplace where the enemy might attack.

Mrs. Roosevelt did not like the idea of war, but she believed that this war had to be fought. She said, "It is not enough to win the fight. We must win that for which we fight—the triumph of all people who believe that the people of this world are worthy of freedom." The first lady liked the idea of a United Nations, an organization that would bring leaders of the world together to talk out their disagreements instead of going to war.

In 1944, Roosevelt won a fourth term as president, but died just three months after his inauguration. Now Eleanor was on her own. She was not sure what she would do. She had been first lady for 12 long years. Instead of just retiring, however, she decided to dedicate her life to world peace.

Harry Truman was the new president. His wife, Bess Wallace, was a quiet woman who had just as much influence over her husband as Eleanor had had over Franklin. Bess Truman was not interested in being as public as Eleanor, but she and President Truman liked Eleanor very much. In 1945, President Truman decided to make Mrs. Roosevelt the U.S. delegate to the new United Nations.

Eleanor lived in New York City and went to work every day at the United Nations. She again traveled around the globe and visited many countries that she had not seen before. Some people thought she should run for political office. However, Eleanor said she didn't want to because "it is wonderful to feel free." At the United Nations, however, she did get involved in politics. Her most famous work was as chairperson of the Commission on Human Rights. She helped create *The Declaration of Human Rights,* a document that listed what every country should give its citizens and what they deserved as human beings. Now many people called Eleanor Roosevelt "first lady of the world."

In 1962, Eleanor Roosevelt became ill while making a speech. A concerned friend said that she should not have spoken. Just then a little girl offered Mrs. Roosevelt some flowers. Mrs. Roosevelt then turned to her friend and said, "You see, I had to come. I was expected." Every person, no matter how small, was important to Eleanor Roosevelt. Because she so wanted to help others and to help her country and the world, Mrs. Roosevelt did not want to slow down. But she became even more seriously ill and died later that year.

Eleanor Roosevelt changed the role of first lady in the twentieth century. She also changed herself from a shy and frightened girl to a brave woman. As she once said, "Nobody can make you feel bad about yourself unless you let them."

Only 31 years old on the day she became first lady—January 20, 1961—Jacqueline Kennedy celebrates her husband's inauguration as thirty-fifth president of the United States with him at her side.

6

Jacqueline Kennedy

*I*n 1961, John F. Kennedy, America's youngest president, was inaugurated. More women who had once been first ladies or who would someday be first ladies attended this inauguration than had ever attended before. Future First Ladies Lady Bird Johnson, Pat Nixon, and Betty Ford joined former First Ladies Edith Wilson, Eleanor Roosevelt, Bess Truman, and Mamie Eisenhower. However, that day, attention was centered not on these women but on the new first lady, one of the youngest ever. Jacqueline Bouvier Kennedy was unlike any other first lady, and she became one of the most famous women in the world.

Jacqueline, the first first lady born in the twentieth century, was born July 28, 1929, on Long Island, New York. Her father, John Bouvier, worked as a

Proudly wearing her horseback riding ribbon, young Jacqueline holds hands with her father, John Bouvier, at the Long Island Horse Show in 1935.

stockbroker who helped people invest their money. Her mother, Janet Lee, loved animals, especially horses, and was one of the best women horseback riders in the United States. As a little girl, Jacqueline learned to ride horses, too, and won many awards.

Jacqueline grew up in New York City where she enjoyed visiting art and history museums and learning about different countries and their cultures. She also studied ballet, and liked to paint and draw. What she loved most was reading for long hours and writing. One of her poems was about walking alone on the beach in the fall:

> I love walking on the angry shore,
> To watch the angry sea;
> Where summer people were
> before,
> But now there's only me.

Jacqueline enjoyed spending time alone. She came to know herself well, and she did not worry if she was alone. Jacqueline was a straight-A student. The woman in charge of her school said that Miss Bouvier had "the most inquiring mind we'd had in the school in thirty-five years."

In 1940, when she was 11 years old, Jacqueline went with her sister and mother for her first tour of the White House. She later said, "I was strangely let down by the White House. It seemed rather bleak; there was nothing in the way of a booklet to take away, nothing to teach one more about that great house and the presidents who had lived there."

After high school, Jacqueline wanted to see more of the world. When she was in her third year of college at Vassar, she decided to live in Paris. (The Bouviers were of French origin, and Jacqueline was especially interested in the French culture. She learned to speak French well, and also studied Spanish and Italian.) While in France, she decided to tour Europe with her sister, Lee, who was her best friend.

While in Europe, Jacqueline met England's famous prime minister, Winston Churchill. She also saw a concentration camp where many thousands of Jewish people had been killed by Adolf Hitler during World War II. When she visited the famous art specialist Barnard Berenson, he told her, "The only way to exist happily is to love your work." Living in another country enabled Jacqueline to experience many new things.

When she finished college, Jacqueline became a reporter for a newspaper in Washington. She wrote a column, "The Inquiring Cameragirl," that appeared in the paper on a regular basis. For this column, Miss Bouvier would ask several people the same question. Then she would take their pictures, which would appear in the paper with their answers. She asked questions such as "Are men braver than women?" Jacqueline also wanted to write a children's book about the White House, but told another reporter that "trying to write anything original about the White House is like asking for the moon."

While working for the newspaper, Jacqueline met John F. Kennedy, a young senator from Massachusetts who had not yet been married. Because their work kept them traveling so much, they saw one another only when time permitted. Nevertheless, in September 1953, they married.

As a senator's wife, Jacqueline was active in her husband's political life and came to his office to work for him. Her language skills proved helpful because she could answer the mail he received from people who did not know how to write in English. When the senator had to learn more about the country of Vietnam, Jacqueline translated many French documents into English for him. She and John, whose nickname was Jack, shared an interest in history and reading.

When Senator Kennedy ran for president in 1960, Jacqueline helped in his campaign. During the campaign, she saw the terrible poverty of coal miners and their families in West Virginia. Jacqueline hoped to do something as first lady to help them. She made speeches for her husband and appeared on television talking about why Jack would be a good president. She wrote a second newspaper column, "Campaign Wife." In this column she gave her ideas on political problems and told what her husband was doing on the campaign. Mrs. Kennedy often spoke to people in their native languages—Spanish, Polish, French. With her help, Senator Kennedy won the election.

Jacqueline Kennedy was unlike any other first lady. For example, the two first ladies who had come just before her, Bess Truman and Mamie Eisenhower, were old enough to be her mother. Bess and Mamie liked to play cards and stay at home. They often gave their husbands opinions on speeches and decisions, but only in private. They did not travel much and were not often in the press. Jacqueline Kennedy was quite different from these two former first ladies.

Jacqueline was the third youngest woman to become first lady. (Only Julia Tyler and Frances Cleveland had been younger.) She was also one of the few first ladies to have young children in the White House. An attractive woman who dressed in modern and youthful clothes, Mrs. Kennedy was active in sports. She liked modern art and jazz music. All of this made her one of the most popular first ladies in history. The American people liked to watch the TV news to hear about the stylish first lady. Many women copied her hairstyle, fashions, and entertaining style.

However, more than art, jazz, sports, and clothes, Mrs. Kennedy enjoyed the work she did as first lady. When she looked through the White House, she still saw no more historic furnishings than she had as an

11-year-old child when she took her first tour there. So, Jacqueline decided that she would try and return to the White House the old furniture used by past presidents. She wanted to make the rooms of the White House look as they once had.

She said that "presidents' wives have an obligation to contribute something. I'd feel badly if I had lived here for four years and hadn't done anything for the house. Everything in the White House must have a reason for being there. It must be restored and that has nothing to do with decoration." She asked, "Why shouldn't the White House inspire people, make them proud of their country's heritage?" She believed that the White House should represent "American excellence."

Daily, Mrs. Kennedy worked on her restoration project. She went through old government buildings and looked for White House furniture. She asked antique experts to help her find old furniture that might be in other homes or museums. She asked citizens who had furnishings or other items from the White House to send these back so they could be displayed.

As she worked on her project, Mrs. Kennedy also remembered how as a child she thought that the White House should offer a book to visitors. So, she began to write *The White House: An Historic Guide*. This book was easy enough for children to read, but it also interested adults. When the book was finished, White House guides sold it, and Mrs. Kennedy used the money to buy more important items for the White House and keep the restoration going. She used no government money as she restored this famous dwelling place of presidents.

*Treated like royalty in India, Mrs. Kennedy (in white dress)
rides atop an elephant along with her sister, Lee Radziwell.*

When she was almost finished with her project, Mrs.
Kennedy took the United States on a tour of the restored
rooms on a special television show called "A Tour of the
White House with Mrs. John F. Kennedy." Three out of
every four Americans watched the program.

The TV show was translated into different languages
and shown all over the world. This helped make
Jacqueline Kennedy one of the most international of first
ladies. Her reputation grew when she traveled to countries such as France, Austria, England, Italy, Greece,
Mexico, Venezuela, India, and Pakistan. In India and
Pakistan, the people treated her like an American queen.

Mrs. Kennedy also worked on many other projects
that had to do with the arts and history. When some
important old buildings around Lafayette Square—the
park across the street from the White House—were
going to be torn down, she prevented the demolition.

Jacqueline helped convince the French government to lend the "Mona Lisa" to America. The painting had never left its French museum, but because of Mrs. Kennedy, it came to the United States. She also got people interested in helping and giving money to build a place in Washington where the performing arts could be seen. President Eisenhower had suggested the idea of this national cultural center. Later, when it was finished, this building was named "The John F. Kennedy Center for the Performing Arts" after her husband. Today, people enjoy concerts, plays, operas, and ballets there. Mrs. Kennedy said the building would be "a living symbol for our national appreciation and pride in the arts."

Mrs. Kennedy also remembered the miners of West Virginia. She bought special glasses for the White House that were made by the poor people there. She would not accept more expensive glasses because she wanted to help the miners. She even let the factory in West Virginia sell glasses just like hers as "White House Glassware." In the White House, the two young Kennedy children, Caroline and John, lived quietly with their parents. Mrs. Kennedy put in a playground for them on the lawn, and Caroline went to a special kindergarten on the top floor of the mansion. Mrs. Kennedy always spent time with her children and tried to give them a normal life.

Mrs. Kennedy cared about children. Whenever she went to a foreign country, she brought a gift for the children of that land. In the White House, she started a series of musical concerts for children. She also invited foreign students who were in America to visit the White House.

With the president, Mrs. Kennedy shared an interest in politics. She felt strongly about his dreams for American space exploration, civil rights for African-Americans, and the Alliance for Progress—a special program to help South American countries with education, medicine, and housing.

Jacqueline hoped that America—like France, Greece, and several other countries—would someday have a Department of the Arts, with a cabinet member in charge. "Our contemporary artists—in all the media," she said, "have excited the world." She added that it was "sad that we couldn't help" these artists more.

Although she was not as interested in politics as Eleanor Roosevelt had been, Mrs. Kennedy was good friends with some of the cabinet members, senators, and members of Congress. She was able to get a special law passed to help keep the White House protected for all times to come. She also talked to members of Congress, and got money from the government to help save some ancient temples in Egypt.

Mrs. Kennedy was with the president when he was shot on a political trip to Texas on November 22, 1963. He died the same day. Although the entire world was saddened and shocked by this, Mrs. Kennedy stayed calm throughout the terrible event and throughout the funeral for the president.

Afterward, Mrs. Kennedy moved with her children to New York, where she was able to live more privately. Five years later, she married Aristotle Onassis, an intelligent man who worked in the Greek shipping business. He and Jacqueline shared an interest in the Mediterranean Sea and the cultures around it. He was very kind to her children, and they enjoyed him.

Jacqueline continued her interests in art, photography, ballet, theater, architecture, and history. In New York, she helped save many beautiful old buildings, like Grand Central Station, that other people wanted to tear down.

After Mr. Onassis died in 1975, Jacqueline decided to go back to work. More than 30 years had passed since she had worked as a reporter. But books had always been her great love, so she became an editor and helped people write them, from the first idea for the book to the finished product.

Today, Jacqueline lives like other private citizens. Her children, John and Caroline, have become lawyers. Caroline is also a writer, and is now a mother. The family remains close.

Jacqueline Kennedy Onassis has made America aware of its own talents. She believes that American artists of all kinds—writers, painters, photographers, dancers, actors, singers, sculptors, poets, and musicians—are as important as those from any other country. She once said that "the artist should be honored by society," and that her proudest work as first lady was to "call attention to what was finest in America, what should be esteemed and honored."

Now a grandmother, Mrs. Onassis remains close to the large Kennedy family. Here she enjoys a party with her brother-in-law, Senator Edward M. Kennedy of Massachusetts.

Doing her part to keep America beautiful, Lady Bird Johnson helps to plant a tree in Washington.

7
Lady Bird Johnson

_M_any of the new ideas of the 1960s clashed with the old ideas of preceding decades. Most people seemed to agree on one new idea, however—the need to protect our land. One woman in the sixties helped make America aware of pollution, the destruction of our land, and the need to protect natural beauty. Even her name—Lady Bird Johnson—seemed to remind people of the natural world.

Mrs. Johnson's real name is Claudia. But just a short time after Claudia Taylor was born in Texas on December 22, 1912, her nursemaid said she looked "as pretty as a lady bird." The nickname stayed with her.

Her mother died when she was young, and little Lady Bird Taylor lived part time with her aunt in Alabama. She enjoyed walking through the beautiful forests beneath the hanging moss trees. She spent many hours playing by herself in the natural setting, and she loved the "drifts of magnolia all through the woods in the spring—and the daffodils in the yard." When the first daffodil of spring bloomed, Lady Bird said, "I would have a little ceremony, all by myself, and name it the queen."

At the University of Texas, Miss Taylor earned a degree in history, but she attended the university a fifth year to study journalism. She explained that she did this because "people in the press went more places and met more interesting people, and had more exciting things happen to them." She then got a job as a reporter for the *Daily Texan*.

Then Miss Taylor returned to school to study business. Her career plans came to a halt, however, when she met the tall and hardworking Lyndon Baines Johnson, often called LBJ. LBJ worked in the office of a United States congressman in Washington. After their first date Lyndon asked Lady Bird to marry him. She accepted and they wed in 1934. Soon, they had two daughters, Lynda and Luci.

Not long afterward, Mr. Johnson ran for Congress himself. Lady Bird helped pay for the expensive campaign by borrowing money from her father. She also campaigned hard for Lyndon, and he won. As a congressional wife, Lady Bird Johnson wrote excitedly in her diary. "I went to my first (will it be my last and only!?!) Dinner at the White House!"

Mrs. Johnson was deeply impressed by Mrs. Roosevelt, who was then first lady in the White House.

Lady Bird and Lyndon Baines Johnson (1908-1973) embrace in front of the U.S. Capitol, where LBJ would rise to power as a congressman and senator.

At this time Eleanor Roosevelt was trying to get better housing for the poor people of Washington who lived in slums. Eleanor had first seen these slums when Ellen Wilson—the first wife of Woodrow Wilson—was first lady. Back then, when Eleanor went with Mrs. Wilson to see the slums, she was just the wife of a cabinet member. She never thought she would be first lady herself someday and would be able to help these people. Now, Mrs. Johnson followed Mrs. Roosevelt as she fought for better housing, never thinking that she herself would someday be first lady.

When World War II started, Congressman Johnson joined the naval reserves of the armed forces. Lady Bird

Johnson took over the running of his congressional office. She also invested money in a radio station. Even though she was sometimes frightened by these new responsibilities, Lady Bird Johnson went ahead and did things. Because of this, she said, "I learned I could handle things if I tried hard enough and I could make a living. It was a good thing to know, and it gave me an increasing sense of self-reliance and self-esteem."

When the citizens of Texas elected LBJ to the Senate in 1948, Lady Bird continued to learn about politics through Sam Rayburn, Speaker of the House of Representatives, who was in charge of directing the members of Congress. He told Mrs. Johnson that "your friendship for me is one of the most heartening things in my life."

After Senator Johnson became majority leader in the Senate, he had a heart attack. As he got well, Mrs. Johnson moved into a room next to his in the hospital and helped by again running his office. She also became active in an organization called "Ladies of the Senate." These women donated their time to charitable causes. When the group met, Lady Bird brought cookies in the shape of Texas. During this time she also took classes on making speeches and language.

Lady Bird Johnson said she "liked to get to know the wives of Lyndon's colleagues." In this way, she became friends with Jacqueline Kennedy, Pat Nixon, and Betty Ford, all of whom, like her, would someday become first ladies.

When the Democratic convention chose LBJ to run as vice-president with presidential candidate John F.

Kennedy in 1960, Mrs. Johnson made many political campaign speeches. In the South, she reached out to people of all races, even though prejudiced people were angry about this. As second lady, Mrs. Johnson helped Mrs. Kennedy entertain large groups and also traveled around the world with the vice-president.

After the assassination of President Kennedy in 1963, Vice-President Johnson became president, and Lady Bird suddenly found herself first lady.

Often, first ladies learn from their predecessors, those who came before them. Lady Bird loved history, especially the history of the White House, and she frequently read about the other first ladies. She said she always liked Dolley Madison because "she enjoyed her role." Mrs. Johnson most vividly remembered her years as a congressional wife while Eleanor Roosevelt was first lady and the things that Eleanor stood for. Lady Bird thought that a first lady must do "what makes her heart sing" and that her own work must "emerge in deeds not words."

On her desk, Lady Bird kept a small sign that said "Can Do." She told young women graduating from college in the sixties that they should try to balance their lives between being wives and mothers and working in other jobs. "In almost every sphere, the influence of women is increasing," she said in 1964. The first lady held special lunch meetings for women of achievement in different areas of interest. They were called "Women Do-er" luncheons and everyone present would discuss the day's topic.

"The War on Poverty," one of President Johnson's

Reading here to a group of children, Lady Bird actively participated in the Head Start program, which began in 1964.

most famous plans, was a group of programs that helped poor Americans. The one called Head Start interested Mrs. Johnson the most. She became its national chairperson. Head Start gave young children medical care, reading skills, and other educational help before they went to school. Lady Bird went to many rural areas of America to see how Head Start was working and returned to tell the president.

In 1964, when LBJ ran for a full term as president, his wife did something no candidate's wife had ever done. She made a special trip on a train called "The Lady Bird Special" and went through the southern states. From the back platform of the caboose, Mrs.

Johnson spoke to crowds gathered in train stations. Some people didn't like her talking about the new laws recognizing the equality of citizens of all races, but she bravely continued to do so.

When LBJ won the election, Lady Bird began her greatest work as first lady by helping to care for the earth and its natural beauty. In ceremonies all across America, she beautified the country by planting many trees, flowers, bushes, and shrubbery. She even helped plant two million daffodils in Washington!

All aboard the Johnson campaign as Lady Bird makes an October 1964 whistle stop in Raleigh, North Carolina.

However, Lady Bird felt that beautification, the name of her project, was more than making streets and towns pretty. She wanted to help people in rundown areas of cities take pride in their communities. Thus, urban renewal began. Remembering how she had followed Eleanor Roosevelt in Washington's slum areas, Lady Bird finally helped in beautifying the slums. To Mrs. Johnson, beautification was something that big companies could help with by providing money and volunteers to create new parks and town greens and to fix up places like gas stations. She hoped many Americans would also learn about nature by visiting the nation's many national parks.

Finally, she believed that preserving and protecting the land for the future was very important. "We have misused our resources," she said, "but we haven't destroyed them. It is late. It is fortunately not too late." Lady Bird believed that every American could help a little by picking up litter, keeping public places clean, and planting trees and flowers. Perhaps the most important thing Lady Bird Johnson did was to help pass a national law that removed distracting signs and billboards from highways. The bill was nicknamed "Lady Bird's Bill."

Mrs. Johnson thought that her political role was "to help my husband do his job." Her husband always told her about his work, and many times she helped him by writing part of his speeches or by talking to other politicians for him. He could always turn to her for advice and comfort. This was especially needed by LBJ because of the Vietnam War that America was fighting in Asia.

This war brought a painful time to the United States. The country entered the war to help Vietnam resist communism. Through the years the United States sent more and more soldiers and money to Southeast Asia. In the middle of the 1960s some people believed strongly that America should stop the war because so many American soldiers were being killed. Others thought America should stay in Vietnam and keep fighting communism. This disagreement got worse, and many people in the United States began to protest. Because Lady Bird's husband was president, some people protested events that she attended.

In 1968, LBJ had to decide if he wanted to run for president again. Lady Bird told him that he must make the decision himself, but that she wanted to move back to Texas so he could finally relax. In March, LBJ told the United States by television that he would not run for re-election. Before they left the White House, however, the country honored the first lady for her work for the environment by setting aside a special area in Washington where daffodils and dogwood trees were planted. The government named this area the "Lady Bird Johnson Park."

Lyndon and Lady Bird Johnson returned to their famous LBJ Ranch in Austin, Texas. There they worked together on planning the presidential library and museum. Here the important papers from LBJ and Lady Bird's lives and work are kept for people to study. Also, the museum displays for visitors many of the personal things and the gifts given to the Johnsons.

Even after LBJ died in 1973, Mrs. Johnson worked to beautify her own community. She helped put hike and bike trails in the town park, along the river. She also ran her radio and television stations, called "KLBJ." Mrs. Johnson still lives in Texas, and continues her interest in projects that help the environment.

One of the greatest works that Lady Bird Johnson did after she left the White House was to begin the National Wildflower Research Center. The various regions of America have different flowers that grow wild. Mrs. Johnson's project helps to keep wildflowers blooming, and allows scientists to study them.

Even though her years as first lady were marked with America's troubles in Vietnam and at home, Lady Bird Johnson helped the nation work to improve conditions for all people. She has said that even a war "does not give us a free ticket not to try and work on bettering the things in this country that we can better. I think we must keep our eyes and our hearts and our energies fixed on constructive aims."

8

Pat Nixon

*D*uring the 1950s and 1960s, America feared that the biggest communist countries, the Soviet Union and the People's Republic of China, would someday try and take over our form of government. Many Americans did not trust the Soviet and Chinese leaders and those leaders did not trust Americans.

In the 1970s, President Richard Nixon participated in what was called détente, the beginning of our friendship with the Soviet Union and the People's Republic of China. During this time, his wife, Pat Ryan Nixon, helped the people of those lands begin to understand Americans. Pat reached out to the people, on a person-to-person basis, a practice called personal diplomacy.

Born as Thelma Catherine Ryan on March 16, 1912, Pat was given her nickname because she was born just a few hours before St. Patrick's Day. Pat's father, Will, was Irish, and her mother had been born in Germany and then immigrated to the United States.

Pat's father worked in the coal mines of Nevada. Soon after her birth, the family moved to California, where Will became a farmer. Here, Pat and her two brothers worked the land every day, planting and taking care of vegetables and fruits.

As a young girl, Pat enjoyed going to the beach and playing with her friends, who called her Buddy. When her mother became sick, Pat took care of her. She cooked and cleaned and did farm chores. When her mother died and her father became sick, Pat worked even harder. But she never complained. She even helped her brothers with their schoolwork. Her dream was to get a college education.

To save money for college, Pat took jobs besides her farm work. Even when she went to Fullerton Junior College, she worked. In the early morning, she cleaned the steps of the bank; during the day, she worked as a teller in the bank. Despite all this work, she was still an excellent student. One of her teachers said, "In any type of occupation requiring the meeting of the public, Pat will be a great success."

Pat Ryan wanted to see the world. She did not want to get married because she said she "had not yet lived." Pat was adventurous: she took flying lessons; she drove a couple in their car across America, from the West to the East Coast. In New York, she modeled and worked in a hospital, where sick children liked her care. Pat even helped some of them sneak off to go sledding on a near-by hill. When she went to a meeting for hospital workers, she heard First Lady Eleanor Roosevelt speak. Pat told her brothers that "the world is just what we make it—so let's make ours a grand one."

When she returned to California, Pat finished her college education. To earn money she worked as a clerk

As a young woman, Pat Ryan worked hard for everything she received, including a degree from the University of Southern California.

in a department store, as a professor's helper, and as an actress. After graduating from college, she became a teacher and was especially kind to students from Mexico who had problems with English. She helped students become involved in many after-school activities.

Pat Ryan was also involved in the community of Whittier, where she taught. While working on a play called *The Dark Tower* she met Richard Nixon, a lawyer who lived nearby. She told friends, "He's going to be president someday." The two fell in love, and Dick told Pat that she was "destined to be a great lady." They married in 1940.

During World War II, when Dick got a job in the government, the Nixons moved to Washington. There, Pat worked as an economist. She assisted small businesses as they tried to keep going in the wartime economy.

As a young congressional family, the Nixons enjoy a bicycle ride around Washington's Tidal Basin.

When Dick joined the navy, Pat worked as an economist in California.

After the war ended, Nixon ran for Congress in 1946. Pat helped by giving his campaign the money her father had left her when he died. She wrote and typed campaign brochures that told about Dick's ideas. Just hours after her daughter, Tricia, was born, Pat was back at the office, reading important information for Dick's campaign. When he won, they moved to Washington. There, another daughter, Julie, was born to the Nixons.

The California citizens elected Nixon their senator in 1950. Pat worked in his senate office, sometimes writing his letters to people who wrote asking Dick for help. Two years later, the Republican convention selected Richard Nixon to run as the candidate for vice-president with the presidential candidate, Dwight D. Eisenhower.

Mrs. Nixon became active in the presidential campaign. She drove all over the country and talked to voters, especially women. Pat Nixon thought women needed to learn about politics. So she went to many gatherings of women voters. She encouraged them to volunteer their time to work for the candidates they supported.

When her husband was elected vice-president, Pat became the most active second lady up to that time. She traveled with him all over the world. They visited foreign countries as a team. Whenever she went somewhere, Pat Nixon visited hospitals, schools, and other places where she could talk to everyday people and learn about their lives and problems. Pat and Dick went to Africa along with African-American leader Martin Luther King, Jr., and his wife, Coretta. In the Soviet Union she talked about missiles with Nikita Khrushchev, the leader of that country. In Venezuela, angry citizens threw rocks at Pat's car because they opposed the United States. However, Pat stayed calm and was friendly even to the angry citizens. When she returned to the United States after this trip, Pat Nixon was famous.

When President Eisenhower became sick, the Nixons attended many events for the Eisenhowers. Pat and Mamie were friends, but Mrs. Nixon spoke out about politics more than the first lady did and always tried to bring attention to the work of women, even in foreign countries. "Everywhere I go," she said, "I help women." One magazine said she was "one of the country's most remarkable women."

When Nixon ran for president against Kennedy in 1960, Pat Nixon was again very active. People wore buttons that said, "Pat Nixon for First Lady." One

Vice-President Richard Nixon reads a Christmas story to his daughters, Julie and Tricia (standing), with Pat and Checkers listening in.

brochure said, "When you elect a president, you are also electing a first lady. She represents America to all the world. Pat Nixon is uniquely qualified." Pat talked about important issues and said her volunteer work was "reflective of women all across America taking an active part, not only in political life, but all activities. There was a day when they stayed home, but they have emerged as volunteers."

Nixon lost the election, and Pat had mixed feelings. She wanted him to win, but she was also happy to be away from politics. She wanted a private life with her two daughters. So, the family lived in California and then New York City. Pat Nixon did volunteer work and enjoyed life. She did not want Dick to go back into politics, but when he ran for president again in 1968, she worked for him.

This time, Nixon won the presidential election, and Pat was now first lady. The Vietnam War and protests about it were still going on, so Mrs. Nixon decided that her work as first lady should not be in the newspapers as much as that of others, such as Eleanor Roosevelt and Lady Bird Johnson. However, she worked on many different projects. One of them was continuing the work, started by Jacqueline Kennedy, of restoring the White House.

Mrs. Nixon believed that the White House belonged to all Americans. She started tours for blind and deaf visitors, as well as for those who were handicapped and needed special help getting around. For those who did not speak English, she had special brochures about the White House printed in foreign languages. In the evening and on certain days, the White House was closed to visitors, so Mrs. Nixon lit it up at night so the building could be seen clearly from the outside all the time. In the spring and fall, she let visitors go through the beautiful gardens for the first time. At Christmas she had special night tours so people who had to work during the day could see the holiday decorations.

Sometimes, Pat even went downstairs and surprised visitors by showing them around. Once a little boy didn't think she lived there because he didn't see her washing machine. The first lady took him by the hand and brought him down the long hallways and up the stairs. Finally they came to the laundry room, and he saw her washing machine. Now he believed!

One reporter who wrote about Mrs. Nixon as well as

many other first ladies said Pat "was the warmest first lady I covered and the one who loved people the most. She is concerned about people's feelings, a very strong woman, and sometimes a very stubborn woman. She never forgets her days of poverty."

Even though she was not often in the news, Pat Nixon made an impression on the everyday people who met her, whether in the White House or on her many trips. For many hours each day she answered the letters that citizens wrote her.

One project on which Mrs. Nixon worked hard was promoting the practice of people volunteering their time to help others. "Our success as a nation," she said, "depends upon our willingness to give generously of ourselves for the welfare and enrichment of the lives of others."

Whenever she traveled around the United States, Pat always went to places run by volunteers—community gardens, centers for blind people, exercise halls for poor children. Mrs. Nixon said volunteerism "can often accomplish things that legislation alone cannot. This is where I think I can help, encouraging what my husband has called those 'small, splendid efforts' of people trying to make life better for others."

If she read or heard about a volunteer project, Mrs. Nixon always sent a letter to encourage the effort. She also invited to the White House volunteer groups that had formed to help solve a community problem.

A program called Legacy of the Parks also interested Pat Nixon. This program took parks that the government in Washington had been caring for and gave them to states for use by people as recreational areas.

Pat Nixon traveled to more foreign countries than any

other first lady in history. When she went to Vietnam, Pat Nixon became the first first lady since Eleanor Roosevelt to go into a war zone. Without the president, she went to three African countries, talked with their leaders, and greeted the people with her personal diplomacy. She even wore a native costume and turban.

When she heard about an earthquake in Peru, Pat Nixon got in touch with American volunteer groups who donated food, clothes, and money. Then she flew to Peru with two planeloads of goods. She went into dangerous mountain areas to see what the people hurt by the earthquake needed. She told the South Americans that "the people of all the Americas are one family."

When President Nixon made his historic visits to the Soviet Union and China, Pat went along. In China, the reporters of the world followed Pat in her famous

In earthquake-rocked Peru, first lady Pat Nixon climbs amid the rubble.

red coat. She spent her days visiting people's homes, schools, workplaces, farms, subways, stores, and theaters. She said of her travels, "These were journeys for peace." Pat Nixon said that her proudest work as first lady was to "establish friendships in Third World and communist countries for the United States."

In 1972, the Republican party nominated President Nixon for a second term. Pat Nixon addressed the national political convention that selected her husband as the presidential candidate. After the convention, she campaigned in almost every state.

At the time, Pat did not know that some men who worked for the president had lied. They were part of a group that had broken into offices of the Democratic party in the Watergate building in Washington to get information. When newspapers discovered this, they called the problem "Watergate." How much the president knew was uncertain. Some said he told the men to withhold information, but he said he did not do so. However, when the press found out that he had made tape recordings of his telephone calls, Congress started an investigation. This caused great trouble for President Nixon. Because Congress might impeach him, that is, ask him to leave the presidency, Nixon resigned on August 9, 1974.

This was a sad day for Pat Nixon. However, as she always had, she found strength inside herself. She calmly left the White House with her head high.

The Nixons retired to Casa Pacifica, their home overlooking the Pacific Ocean in San Clemente, California. In 1976, Pat Nixon suffered a stroke, the same illness that had affected Nellie Taft. However, through hard work in physical therapy she got a bit

116

better every day and fully recovered. In 1981, the Nixons moved to New York City and then to New Jersey to be near their daughters and grandchildren.

Pat Nixon is a good example of how a person can learn to overcome many difficult situations by choosing to think positively about a problem. No matter what was happening, Mrs. Nixon said, "I always tried my best." By staying calm she was able to get through problems. "I learned a long time ago that if I worry about what might happen," she said, "my energies are sapped." She always sees the good in people. She once said that "some people are not as friendly as others. The main thing is that you treat them in a friendly fashion rather than becoming like them. They will change for the better. That is true all through life."

On August 9, 1974, the day her husband resigned his presidency, Pat kisses her old friend and neighbor Betty Ford goodbye, as the Nixons prepare to board the helicopter that will take them away from the White House.

The future first lady, Betty Bloomer, at about age 20

9
Betty Ford

*I*n the 1970s, the national movement for equal rights for women focused on passing an addition to the Constitution, called the Equal Rights Amendment, or the ERA. More women were seeking higher educations and jobs that had for many years been given only to men. These women wanted to make sure that they had the same rights as men and that they received the same pay when they did the same job. One person who supported the ERA and spoke often about it was the first lady, Betty Ford.

Other first ladies—Abigail Adams, Nellie Taft, Florence Harding, Eleanor Roosevelt, Lady Bird Johnson, and Pat Nixon—had supported women's rights. Betty Ford, however, was not afraid to support women by doing and saying things that no other presidents' wives had ever dared to do.

She was born as Elizabeth Anne Bloomer in Chicago, Illinois on April 8, 1918, but always had the nickname Betty. When she was still little, the Bloomer family moved to Grand Rapids, Michigan.

As a young girl, Betty admired her grandmother, Anna Bloomer, because she had worked for a living. The first lady, Eleanor Roosevelt, became Betty's role model because as Betty said, "I really liked the idea that a woman was finally speaking out and expressing herself rather than just expressing the views of her husband. That seemed healthy to me." From an early age, Betty Bloomer loved to dance. She took all kinds of dance lessons, but found her happiness in modern dance because of its freedom of movement. As a teenager she worked to earn her own money. After her Saturday-morning job as a model in a department store, Betty taught dance to other young people. She rented a friend's basement, hired a piano player, and showed children how to do dances like the fox-trot and Big Apple.

Betty's father was a traveling salesman. When he died suddenly, her mother, Hortense, supported the family by working in real estate. Betty wanted to go to a school for dance. For two summers she attended Bennington College in Vermont and studied with Martha Graham, one of the world's most famous modern dance teachers.

Soon after, at the age of 20, Betty moved to New York City and studied again with Martha Graham in her regular studio. She loved eating at the delicatessens and riding on the subway. To make money, she worked for a famous modeling agency, the Powers Agency. She also

120

performed with Martha Graham's dance company in Carnegie Hall.

When her mother visited Betty, however, she asked her to come back to Michigan for a while instead of following her career in New York. Then, if Betty still wanted to, she could move back to New York later. Betty returned to Michigan and thought later, "I had made my choice."

Back in Grand Rapids, however, Betty continued with dance. She taught modern dance to poor children in the downtown section of the city and was called "The Martha Graham of Grand Rapids." Soon after, she married a man named Bill Warren.

Because of World War II, Betty and Bill lived in different parts of the country. In Toledo, Ohio, she taught dance at the nearby university. In Syracuse, New York, Betty worked in a frozen-food factory, putting vegetables in boxes. When the couple returned to Grand Rapids, Betty became the executive fashion coordinator for a large department store. There she chose and ordered the women's clothes that the store would sell.

Betty and Bill's marriage ended in divorce. She continued to support herself and and to live by herself in an apartment. Her job took her to places such as New York, the center of the fashion industry.

A year later, Betty met a lawyer named Gerald Ford. They began dating, but Jerry was busy running for Congress. In fact, when they got married in October 1948, he was late for the ceremony, and his shoes were dusty from campaigning all day. One month later, Jerry was elected to Congress.

When Betty Ford first came to Washington, she took classes in public speaking. She also met First Lady Bess Truman and became friends with Lady Bird Johnson and Pat Nixon. Later, when Mamie Eisenhower was first lady, she invited Betty to play cards at the White House. Betty later remembered, "I wasn't socializing much in the middle of the afternoon in the city. I was living in the suburbs raising a family. Not playing cards, but driving to Cub Scouts."

The Fords had four children—Mike, Jack, Steve, and Susan. However, because Congressman Ford was sometimes away from home for weeks at a time, Betty Ford had to often be both a father and mother to the children. She was also involved in volunteer work with the Republican congressional wives. Sometimes this caused problems for Betty as it did for many other American mothers who were also too busy. To help relieve her problems, Mrs. Ford spoke with a psychiatrist. During this same period, as she lifted a kitchen window, Mrs. Ford hurt her shoulder and pinched a nerve. The doctor gave her pills to relieve the pain. Over the years, other doctors would continue to give her pain killers.

Mrs. Ford believed that even though she was no longer working professionally and was now spending time raising a family, she should still keep informed about public affairs and government. Her husband had an important position in Congress as House Minority Leader. (This meant he was the representative of congressional members who belonged to the political party that had fewer members in Congress.) Even though the Fords were Republicans, Betty was close to the president's wife,

Lady Bird Johnson, during the 1960s. She and other congressional wives often discussed issues of the day. Mrs. Ford also helped to bring about the idea of a TV series about the three branches of government.

When Nixon became president, the question of whether Congress would pass the ERA became an issue. The women's movement was now mentioned in the news often. Betty Ford supported the ERA. She remembered how her mother had worked hard. She also remembered a time when she was married to Bill Warren and he had become sick. Betty had had to work and support him for a while. She thought then that if she had had to work to support him for the rest of his life, in fairness she should be paid the same amount as a man who did the same work as she would do.

In 1973, when Nixon's vice-president, Spiro Agnew, resigned, Jerry Ford was chosen to be the new vice-president. This surprised Betty. Mrs. Ford decided that because she was used to speaking her opinions on many issues she would continue to do so, even to reporters. Some of these issues, like her telling how she had seen a psychiatrist, were personal.

When President Nixon resigned in 1974, Betty Ford was even more shocked than before. Suddenly, overnight, she was first lady of the United States. When the new president delivered his inaugural address to the nation he said, "I am indebted to no man and only to one woman, my dear wife, Betty." This was the first time a president ever talked about his wife in an inaugural speech. For herself, Betty said, "I wasn't sure what kind of first lady I would be."

Betty Ford decided that she "wanted to be a good first lady" but that she didn't believe that she "had to do every single thing some previous president's wife had done." She said "I've spent too many years being me. I can't suddenly turn into a princess."

This decision to express herself openly was a new way for first ladies to act. For example, almost all the presidents and their wives shared the same bed when they went to sleep at night, but no first lady had ever mentioned this. Betty Ford did. Her responses to reporters' questions sometimes upset people. Betty Ford did not deny or cover up problems in the the United States. She never thought that young people should use drugs, but she did say that she was not surprised that some did. This was her honest opinion. "When someone asks you

Betty looks on with pride as Chief Justice Warren Burger swears in Gerald R. Ford as the thirty-eighth president of the United States, on August 9, 1974.

Mr. and Mrs. Ford stand in the White House with their children, from left: Jack, Steve, Susan, daughter-in-law Gayle, and Mike.

how you stand on an issue," she said, "you're very foolish to beat around the bush—you just meet yourself going around the bush the other way."

Just one month after becoming first lady, Mrs. Ford learned that she had breast cancer. However, instead of keeping this disease secret as many other first ladies had done about their illnesses, she decided to tell the entire nation.

Within hours, hundreds of thousands of women went to their doctors to see if they had the same kind of cancer. Betty said, "I just cannot stress enough how necessary it is for women to take an active interest in their own health and body." Her courage helped American women become aware of the problem of breast cancer and saved thousands of lives by preventing the illness from getting worse in the women who did have it.

Mrs. Ford said that, "lying in the hospital thinking of all those women going for cancer checkups because of me, I'd come to realize more clearly the power of the woman in the White House. Not my power, but the power of the position, a power which could be used to help."

Helping women became the focus of Betty Ford's role as first lady. She tried to get more women appointed to high political jobs. At special dinners, she often placed an important woman who wanted to work in a high government position next to President Ford so they could talk. One woman she helped to become a cabinet member was Carla Hills, who became secretary of Housing and Urban Development. Mrs. Ford, like Mrs. Nixon, wanted a woman judge chosen for the Supreme Court. However, President Ford chose a man when an opening occurred.

Betty Ford's support of the ERA was her most famous work on behalf of women. In the White House, she telephoned important politicians and asked them to help make the ERA a new law. She made many speeches around the country asking citizens to support the amendment. In one speech she said, "While many opportunities are open to women today, too many are available only to the lucky few. Many barriers continue to block the paths of most women. The ERA will not be an instant solution. It will help knock down those restrictions that have locked women into old stereotypes." Betty Ford got more mail from Americans agreeing with her views on the ERA than from those who disagreed. However, in the 1980s Congress turned down the ERA.

Three days after America's 200th birthday, England's Queen Elizabeth II and her husband, Prince Phillip, join the Fords on the Truman Balcony of the White House.

Another thing that Betty made a point of saying was that women should have a choice about what they wanted to do. She told the American public about how she managed a career for many years, and then had a family. Mrs. Ford knew that being a wife, mother, and homemaker was also a job that others should respect. She said that the country should stop using the expression "just a housewife" and should instead say simply, "a housewife."

The Bicentennial, the 200th anniversary of the signing of the Declaration of Independence, occurred in 1976. During that year, Betty Ford opened several museum exhibits on the history of American women. At the White House she greeted many women's groups who visited Washington. She was also hostess to the Queen of England, who came to visit the White House to celebrate the Bicentennial.

With her background in modern dance, Betty Ford had an interest in the performing arts. She influenced the president to ask Congress for 50 million dollars for the arts. She also influenced him to give her old teacher, Martha Graham, a special Medal of Freedom. She invited many dancers to perform in the White House. When Betty entertained guests, she also used American crafts, such as metal sculptures of cowboys and Native American baskets, as table decorations.

In 1976, Gerald Ford ran for president, but lost to Jimmy Carter. When Betty Ford left the White House, she began to drink a lot of alcohol without realizing how much she was consuming. She was also still taking the drugs that her doctors had prescribed. This combination of drugs and alcohol left her feeling ill. In 1978, her husband and children came to her directly and told Betty that she was suffering from addiction.

Now began the the hardest time of her life. Betty went to a special hospital to learn how to live without alcohol or drugs. Even though she was no longer first lady, Betty decided that she must be honest with America about her addiction. Once again, she helped citizens, especially women. She realized that women consumed alcoholic drinks for different reasons than men did. She let people know that this common problem was nothing to be ashamed about. She encouraged people to get help for their addiction.

After she had helped herself get well, Mrs. Ford decided to help others with the same problem. Near her home in the desert community of Rancho Mirage, California, she raised money for a center to help those addicted to alcohol and drugs conquer their addictions and start new lives. The Betty Ford Center was opened by Betty and Jerry Ford in 1982, with Barbara and George Bush also present.

Betty Ford continues to work at the center named after her and lives in Rancho Mirage. When different political issues come up and people ask her point of view, Betty Ford still gives her honest opinion.

Like every other human being, Betty Ford had suffered problems. As she said, "Life is made up of problems. I can't imagine anyone not having problems." But, as she told one group of high school graduates, they must "trust and believe" in themselves. Betty believes that "each individual makes his own dreams. What is important in our lives is not so much what we have in the way of intelligence or talent but what we do with these gifts."

Betty Ford believes that not only should people help others but they should also be true to their best self. Her definition of happiness is "being flexible and willing to give, understand, love and still keep your own identity."

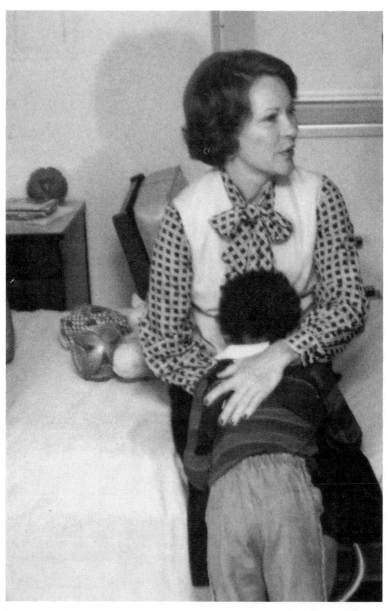

Showing the compassion that would typify her years as first lady, Rosalynn Carter comforts a child in the hospital.

10

Rosalynn Carter

*I*n the late 1970s, many problems affected individual Americans, from young children who had not had proper medical protection to senior citizens who were not sure how to handle their money or what rights they had. Many people—young and old, rich and poor, black and white—have suffered from what is called mental illness. (Mental illness disrupts people's thinking and feelings. Something small can hurt someone for only a short time, or the problem may be a serious one that affects a person for many years.) This embarrasses these people, even though the fault is not always theirs. First Lady Rosalynn Carter tried to help people suffering from mental illness.

Rosalynn Carter was born as Eleanor Rosalynn Smith in Plains, Georgia, on August 18, 1927. At the time Rosalynn grew up, only about 600 people lived in Plains.

Rosalynn grew up in a small white house, which she said was "secure and isolated from the outside world." Around the house, in the red soil of Georgia, grew many colorful flowers, and fruit and nut trees.

Rosalynn had a sister and two brothers. Her mother, known as "Miss Allie," was a rare woman in her place and time because she had earned a college degree. Rosalynn's father, Edgar Smith, was a mechanic, a farmer, and a school bus driver. The people in Plains considered the Smiths lucky because they had their own car. They were not rich, but they were a religious family that participated in church activities. Rosalynn played kick-the-can and set up a play store in the family barn. She made quilts and loved to read.

Rosalynn remembered seeing, as a young girl, pictures of First Ladies Martha Washington and Dolley Madison and thinking they were "women who sat in the White House with their hands clasped in front of them." However, with Eleanor Roosevelt in the White House, Miss Smith became "aware that there was more to being the wife of the president than sitting back in the White House and enjoying the nice life."

Rosalynn was an excellent student. As a third grader she even helped second graders with their math. As a seventh grader, she was excited when a teacher brought in a world map. At that moment she realized "that the boundaries of the world extended beyond our sheltered and isolated community." Rosalynn dreamed of seeing the world someday.

Rosalynn earned her own money by doing shampoos in a beauty shop. She graduated number one in her high

Naval officer Jimmy Carter and his bride, Rosalynn, pose near the marriage altar.

school class, and although she was nervous, Rosalynn delivered her first speech on graduation day. More than anything else, she wanted to attend college. Although her family did not have enough money to send her away to school, Rosalynn worked hard as a student at Georgia Southwestern College, and rode the bus there every morning.

Rosalynn's best friend was a neighbor, Ruth Carter. By the time Rosalynn had graduated from college, Ruth's brother, Jimmy Carter, was a student at the Annapolis Naval Academy. Even though Rosalynn and Jimmy had known each other for some time, they fell in love only when they were older. They agreed to get married after they graduated from college. That happened on July 7, 1946, after World War II ended.

Rosalynn later admitted that she was happy to get out of the small town of Plains. As the wife of a naval officer, she lived in Hawaii, Virginia, Pennsylvania, California, and Connecticut. In Hawaii, Rosalynn even danced the traditional hula. She learned to cook, and took art and music classes. She also had three sons— Jack, Chip and Jeff. She enjoyed the independence she had finally achieved.

When news came that Jimmy's father had died, the family returned to Plains and took over the family businesses, which included a peanut farm. Rosalynn hated the idea of going back to the small town. "I argued. I cried. I even screamed at him," she said later.

However, Mrs. Carter decided to work with Jimmy in the peanut business. She took care of the money side of it, keeping the financial records accurate. "After a few years," she said, "I was explaining some things to him. I knew more about the business on paper than Jimmy did. I knew which parts of the business were profitable, which were not, how much money we had, how much credit, and how much we owed on our debts." This had a great effect on the Carter marriage. "We grew together," said Rosalynn, "as full partners."

Meanwhile, Jimmy became involved in his community. When the citizens of his district elected him to the state legislature in 1963, Rosalynn ran the business in Plains. She also helped him write letters to the people of his district. The Carters were Democrats and supported the civil rights of African-Americans. Many people in Plains did not agree with this viewpoint, and sometimes they vandalized the Carters' property, but the Carters stood up for their beliefs.

Many new and wonderful surprises were in store for Rosalynn. In 1967 she had another child, Amy, her only daughter. Three years later, Jimmy was elected governor of Georgia. Mrs. Carter helped him succeed. She campaigned throughout the entire state, talking to voters everywhere—at tobacco auctions, dog shows, even on shrimp boats.

At a factory, Rosalynn talked with a woman who had to work day and night to support a daughter who was mentally ill. Rosalynn grew concerned that people in Georgia had to live in such terrible situations. When she told Jimmy about her concern, he replied, "We're going to have the best mental health system in the country, and I'm going to put you in charge."

As the governor's wife, Mrs. Carter overcame her fear of public speaking. She visited every mental health hospital in Georgia. She also volunteered to work in a mental health hospital one day a week and to assist a special committee set up by Governor Carter to help the mentally ill of Georgia. This work resulted in improved personal care with the opening of new centers and change in those that already existed.

When Jimmy Carter ran for president in 1976, Rosalynn told the voters that as first lady she would help the mentally ill all across America. Unlike most political wives, Rosalynn campaigned on her own. She and Jimmy did this because they could cover twice as much ground. In three and a half days, for example, Mrs. Carter campaigned in 23 different cities. Wherever she went, Rosalynn always looked for radio station antennae. When she sighted a station, she drove to it and asked if the personnel there wanted to interview her.

Unlike most candidates' wives, Rosalynn also liked to talk about the economy, Congress, and international issues. In one town, she made 12 speeches.

Rosalynn Carter was also the only candidate's wife to make a promise of her own if she became the first lady. "When my husband is elected president," she said, "I want him to establish a Presidential Commission on Mental Health!" When Jimmy became president in 1977, that is exactly what he did.

No first lady had ever treated her role in such a businesslike manner as Rosalynn Carter did. She said, "A first lady is in a position to know the needs of the country and do something about them. She can have real influence. I think that the wives of presidents need to be informed and to speak out on matters that are important to them."

The first lady was put in charge of the new President's Commission on Mental Health. She visited many centers all over the country and talked to doctors and experts to see how to improve the facilities and procedures. She even met with people in Hollywood to ask them to change the way they showed people with mental illness in movies and on television. In meetings across America, the commission invited citizens to give their opinions and to tell their own stories. Many other meetings were held in the White House.

Rosalynn knew that mental illness was not often as terrible as some people thought it sounded. Many times it was just a matter of a person having "the blues," a long period of sadness. However, people needed to talk to doctors and help themselves feel and think better.

Through her work on the commission, Rosalynn learned that mental illness affects one in four American families in some way.

Mrs. Carter's commission suggested that the government pass a new law to improve the community services provided to those suffering from mental illness, and to create new services so everyone who needed help could be reached. She became the only first lady besides Eleanor Roosevelt to testify before Congress.

Mrs. Carter also helped to protect the health of all of America's children against measles. The first lady's goal of immunizing 90 percent of the children was achieved. She also helped the elderly in America by putting together a group of experts to organize and inform senior citizens about the services available to them. She helped develop a brochure that told the elderly about their rights and how to get help. She went to Congress to discuss the Age Discrimination Act, a law that prohibited prejudice against the elderly.

Rosalynn Carter became the only first lady to set up her own business office in the area known as the east wing of the White House. Every morning when she was in Washington, Mrs. Carter walked over to her office, a smaller building attached to the White House. She carried a briefcase filled with work and wore a business suit to the east wing, where many people worked with her to help the American people.

In the morning she often took Amy to a nearby public school. During the rest of the day, Rosalynn worked and studied Spanish. Once a week, she had a special lunch with the president in his office. Mrs. Carter

Between foreign policy discussions with South American leaders in June 1977, Mrs. Carter greets children in Ecuador.

explained why she worked so hard: "My father was a mechanic, and my mother was a seamstress. We were very, very poor, and we worked very hard. I have always worked. I understand people who work for a living."

One of the hardest jobs she did was to be the president's representative on a special mission to Central and South American countries. After many days of meetings with important advisors from the State Department—which deals with affairs in other countries—the first lady visited Jamaica, Costa Rica, Ecuador, Peru, Brazil, Colombia, and Venezuela. There Mrs. Carter talked about serious issues with those countries' leaders.

Mrs. Carter gave a speech about America's policies in each country and talked with leaders about military equipment, the exports of products, stopping the flow of drugs, giving human rights to prisoners, nuclear energy, and weapons. The first lady said, "I am the person closest to the president and if I can explain his policies and let the people of Latin America know of his great interest and friendship, I intend to do so!" After each meeting, Mrs. Carter sent back a daily report to the State Department, and when she returned, she wrote a full report.

Mrs. Carter was also interested in the arts. She hosted the first poetry reading in the White House and the first jazz festival. She helped start the White House Preservation Fund to raise enough money so that when the mansion needed repair, the work could be done. Rosalynn made some changes in the White House. In one room, she put the wood panels of her grandfather's barn on the walls. On the lawn, she had a treehouse built for Amy.

In 1979 some citizens of Iran took Americans living there as hostages. That is, they held the Americans against their will. The new leader of Iran was angry at the United States because it had helped Iran's former leader, the Shah. This was a terrible time for the country. President Carter stayed close to the White House as he tried to free the hostages.

During the hostage crisis, Mrs. Carter again traveled overseas by herself. This time, she went to Thailand. Millions of people who lived in Cambodia were being killed. Some managed to cross the border to Thailand, but had to live in refugee camps. With no medicine and food, thousands were dying of disease.

Rosalynn overcame her shyness for public speaking and campaigned strenuously for her husband's re-election bid.

Mrs. Carter visited the camps, and what she saw shocked her. She picked up a baby who weighed only four pounds; a few minutes later, the baby died.

When she returned to the United States, Rosalynn helped to raise millions of dollars to aid these Cambodians. She made commercials asking Americans for help and hosted special events at the White House. She was responsible for solving part of the crisis.

In 1980 Jimmy Carter ran for another term as president. Rosalynn campaigned almost every day because Jimmy had to stay near the White House. So, the first lady began making the kind of political speeches that the candidate usually does. Even though Jimmy Carter lost the election to Ronald Reagan, Rosalynn Carter had a great celebration. In 1980, Congress passed her special law, The Mental Health Systems Act.

When Rosalynn returned to Georgia, she continued to work on mental health, and on the building of the Carter Center in Atlanta. The center houses important documents and museum items of the Carter presidency, and welcomes international leaders who come to work out problems. The Carters have their offices and an apartment at the Center.

Rosalynn has written a book, *First Lady from Plains*, about her life. Jimmy and Rosalynn wrote their first book together called *Everything to Gain*. This book gives their ideas about how older people can still do many new things with their lives and live healthfully.

The Carters are still active on projects that help people around the world. Sometimes they build houses for the poor with a group called Habitat for Humanity. Rosalynn has also continued Eleanor Roosevelt's work for human rights in foreign countries.

Rosalynn Carter's involvement in politics happened because she had a marriage based on equality. This was a change that was happening in many other American families. "The role of first lady has changed as the role of women has changed, "said Rosalynn Carter. "Women now take professions. I don't think that any man who would be president of the United States would have a wife who would just sit around and do nothing."

In June 1988 ceremonies at the Kremlin in Moscow, Nancy Reagan (holding flowers) walks with Soviet leader Mikhail Gorbachev, his wife Raisa, and President Reagan.

11

Nancy Reagan

*I*n the 1980s, the United States and the Soviet Union finally began to become closer friends. Nuclear weapons frightened the people of both countries. However, these countries had leaders who wanted to work together to stop this danger. The Soviets had Mikhail Gorbachev, and the Americans had President Ronald Reagan. As Reagan met with Gorbachev and got to know him better, Nancy Reagan encouraged this friendship. Like many people, she wanted peace, and she often talked to her husband about it.

Born in New York City in 1921, Nancy Reagan was christened Anne Frances Robbins, but nicknamed Nancy. Her mother, Edith Luckett Robbins, and her father, Kenneth Robbins, divorced shortly after her birth, and she spent her earliest years as a "backstage baby" while her mother pursued a career in the theater. Because Nancy's mother wanted her to have a more normal life than one surrounded by the props of backstage theaters, she took Nancy to live with her aunt, uncle, and cousin in Bethesda, Maryland, which is near Washington, D.C. One Easter, her aunt and uncle took Nancy to the famous Easter egg roll contest held on the White House lawn, when Grace Coolidge was first lady.

Nancy also spent time with her mother when she was working on the stage. She said, "Visits with Mother were wonderful. I loved to dress up in her stage clothes, put on her makeup, and pretend that I was playing her part." When she was eight years old, Nancy went to live in Chicago. Her mother had married a doctor named Loyal Davis who lived there. Dr. Davis was very kind to her, and she was happy when he became her father. Nancy often went to the hospital with him and watched him work.

At a girls' Latin school, Nancy enjoyed learning drama and was the president of the drama club. She was the star of a play called *First Lady*. In 1939, Nancy Davis went to Smith College in Massachusetts to study drama. She graduated during World War II. Afterward, she returned to Chicago and worked at a department store, and then as a nurse's aide in a hospital where she took care of soldiers wounded in the war.

Later, Nancy worked in a United Service Organizations (USO) center where enlisted men rested, ate, and were entertained before going off to war. Later, when one of her mother's friends, an actress named Zasu Pitts, offered Nancy a part in a play on

144

Nancy Davis enjoys an evening out with one of Hollywood's biggest stars, Academy Award winner Clark Gable (1901-1960), who helped her arrange a screen test and contract with his studio, MGM.

Broadway, she moved to New York City. (Broadway is the street in New York where all the great stage theaters are located.) Although Nancy did not have a speaking part in her first play, she did in her second, *Lute Song*. She starred with Mary Martin, a famous actress of the time. Mary Martin later became well-known for playing Peter Pan on stage and on TV.

After working for a few years in New York stage plays and on some television programs, Nancy Davis moved to Hollywood and tried out for Metro-Goldwyn-Mayer, where she began making movies. During this time, she worked with many famous movie stars, and eventually made 11 movies. She lived independently in her own house. But Nancy said that someday, after working, she wanted to have a successful marriage.

*The newlywed
Reagans cut their
wedding cake.*

In 1949, Nancy met an actor named Ronald Reagan. As well as being an actor, Ronald was the president of the Screen Actor's Guild. This organization helped actors with pay and work problems. He and Nancy married on March 4, 1952. Although Nancy loved working as an actress, she became a full-time wife, and later a mother to their children: Maureen, Michael, Patti, and Ron.

As time went on, Ronald's interest in politics grew. When Nixon ran for president in 1960, the Reagans helped his campaign. When the Nixons moved back to California, Pat Nixon got to know Nancy Reagan. Then Ronald changed his political party from

Democrat to Republican. By 1962, Nancy wrote, "Not a day goes by when someone doesn't come to the house and ask Ronnie to run for senator or governor or even president of the United States."

Reagan was elected governor of California in 1966. The campaign helped Nancy become aware of a new problem that many young people were facing. Many teenagers, and even young children, were turning to drug use. These drugs seemed to change the way the young people felt and acted and often damaged their minds and bodies. Mrs. Reagan spoke out against drug abuse and learned how she could help those who used drugs.

As first lady of California, Nancy also became interested in helping the wounded soldiers coming back from the Vietnam War. As Eleanor Roosevelt had done as first lady, Nancy wrote a newspaper column focusing on social issues. Nancy gave her earnings from this column to a group called Families of POW-MIA, which stands for "Prisoners of War Missing in Action." This referred to American soldiers still in Vietnam who were missing and their whereabouts unknown. The organization helped the soldiers' families.

Another of Mrs. Reagan's projects was the Foster Grandparents Program. This organization helped older people who had retired meet young handicapped children who needed special care. The older people gave time and attention to the children, and the children became special youngsters in the older people's lives. Nancy helped the Foster Grandparents Program become popular in the United States, and later when she visited Australia, she started a Foster Grandparents program there.

As an actress and as first lady of California, Nancy Reagan had already had a chance to meet many of the presidents and first ladies. Once, right after they married, the Reagans had performed in front of President Harry Truman. Because her parents were friends of Dwight and Mamie Eisenhower, Nancy also got to meet them. In 1967, Lady Bird Johnson invited Nancy Reagan to the White House. At her first visit to the White House, Mrs. Reagan felt "awed."

After his term as governor ended, Reagan campaigned for the Republican nomination for president in 1976, but President Ford won. However, four years later, in 1980, Reagan ran again and this time won both the Republican nomination and the election. He was inaugurated as the fortieth president in January 1981.

When she first became first lady, Mrs. Reagan said she was "a nester," and began to have the White House repaired, hoping to make it as beautiful as it could be. Mrs. Reagan felt that, as a symbol of the American people, the White House should be in the best condition possible. For this refurbishment project, the American people donated money to help restore the White House. For the first time in a long time, the upstairs private rooms looked as fine as the downstairs public rooms. The doors, the floors, the walls—everything—was fixed and cleaned. Many pieces of furniture, which were works of art, were brought out of storage, restored, and put on display for visitors to enjoy. Everything was fixed and cleaned as it never had been before.

As first lady, Mrs. Reagan tried to help young Americans stay away from or get off drugs. She did this in many ways. In the White House, she held meetings with children who had used drugs and with medical experts. On the tennis courts, she held special tennis games to raise money to fight drug abuse. She talked about drugs on TV and radio shows and was in a music video about harmful drugs. During the halftime of one Super Bowl football game, she appeared in a commercial talking about the drug problem in the United States.

Mrs. Reagan also visited many classrooms all over the country and spoke with young people about the danger of using drugs. When visiting some children in Oakland, California, Mrs. Reagan was asked by a young girl what she should do if someone offered her drugs. Mrs. Reagan said "Just say no!" This became an expression used by other schoolchildren and soon "Just Say No" clubs formed in schools. The "Just Say No" slogan became a powerful symbol of Mrs. Reagan's campaign.

Over the years, thousands of children wrote letters to Mrs. Reagan, thanking her and telling her to continue her work. She has always remembered one special letter and said, "The first time I received a letter saying that I had saved a person's life, I wept. I never dreamed I had the ability to influence people unknown to me."

In addition to her anti-drug work, Mrs. Reagan also used other opportunities to help people. On a visit to Korea with the president in 1983, Nancy learned of two Korean children in need of special heart surgery. The children flew back to the United States with the

Reagans aboard Air Force One, the president's airplane, and Mrs. Reagan helped them go to St. Francis Hospital where they received the care they needed.

Mrs. Reagan also helped Russian pianist Vladimir Feltsman to move from the Soviet Union to the United States. He even played piano recitals at the White House, at the invitation of President and Mrs. Reagan.

Nancy believed that the most important role of the first lady was to be the wife of the president. At times, the news media criticized her for the way she watched out for her husband, but as President Reagan once said, "I'm not sure a man could be a good president without a wife who is willing to express her opinions with frankness." The Reagans worked as a team. Nancy was very good at learning about people's personalities and how they could best help the president.

Just two months after Reagan had become president, someone shot him, and he nearly died. Nancy and the American people were very worried about him. While he recovered in the hospital for several weeks, Mrs. Reagan made sure that his advisors did not push too much work on him too soon. She also made sure that he followed his doctor's orders. She helped him in this same way when he later had surgery for cancer.

During her husband's second presidential term, which began in 1985, Nancy worked harder to fight drugs. Whenever she went to another country with the president, she helped to form anti-drug groups and visited centers where people who had once used drugs met. She became the first first lady to meet with a Roman Catholic pope on her own to talk about such a serious issue.

After surviving an assassination attempt in 1981, President Reagan, a former movie actor, jokingly apologized to Nancy, saying he "forgot to duck" the bullet. Nancy made sure her husband's hospital stay was as pleasant as possible.

After the president signed the Anti-drug Abuse Act of 1986, he turned the pen over to Nancy because she had influenced the passage of this bill. When he talked about drugs to the nation in a presidential speech, Nancy also spoke.

Nancy Reagan hosted one of the most historic events ever held in the White House. She invited the

Nancy became a forceful speaker against the drug problem that plagued the United States in the 1980s, encouraging children to "just say no" to illegal drug use.

wives of leaders of many foreign countries to meet together and talk about the drug problem. She attended another meeting at the United Nations for the wives of international leaders. Finally, she became the only first lady in history to address the United Nations, where she talked about the drug problem.

The idea of a first lady having a special project had developed over the years. In the 1980s other political wives also took on special projects. For example,

Barbara Bush, wife of the vice-president during Reagan's term in office, started literacy programs to teach adults and children to read, and asked people to give help and care to the homeless. When she became first lady in 1989, Mrs. Bush continued this work. She even helped her dog Millie "write" a book that raised money for literacy.

Some felt that perhaps the most important thing Nancy Reagan did was to help her husband become friends with the leader of the Soviet Union, Mikhail Gorbachev. When a Soviet representative met Mrs. Reagan, he told her that she should whisper the word "peace" in her husband's ear every night. "I will," she said, "and I am also going to whisper 'peace' to you." As she later said, "With the world so dangerous, I felt it was ridiculous for these two heavily armed superpowers to be sitting there and not talking to each other."

Finally, the two countries agreed to stop building certain dangerous weapons and to get rid of others. Reagan and Gorbachev signed the INF Treaty (the Intermediate-Range Nuclear Forces Treaty) in the White House in December 1987.

Nancy Reagan left the White House in 1989, after living there for eight years. Only Mamie Eisenhower, Eleanor Roosevelt, and Julia Grant had lived there as long as she had. She felt that the longer she was first lady, the better she became in her role. "As with many jobs," she said, "the more knowledge and experience you gain, the more secure you feel in the position."

Today, Nancy lives with her husband in Los Angeles, California, near their family and friends. Mrs. Reagan is now in charge of The Nancy Reagan Foundation, which helps groups fight drug abuse among children. She is also interested in the building of the new Reagan Presidential Library and Museum. When the building was dedicated in November 1991, Lady Bird Johnson, Pat Nixon, Betty Ford, Rosalynn Carter, and Barbara Bush joined Nancy Reagan for the occasion. This was the largest gathering of former first ladies in history.

Nancy Reagan helped America change its view of first ladies by being a strong person who did not let critics change her role. She explained that "the first lady is first of all a wife. That's the reason she's there. A president has advisors. But no one among those experts is there to look after him as an individual with human needs. It's legitimate for a first lady to look after a president's health and well-being." President Reagan appreciated what all first ladies had done and said, "First ladies aren't elected, and they don't receive a salary. They have mostly been private persons forced to live public lives, and in my book, they've all been heroes."

Bibliography

Anthony, Carl Sferrazza. *First Ladies: The Saga of the Presidents' Wives and Their Power, 1789-1990*. 2 vols. New York: William Morrow, 1990 and 1991.

Carter, Rosalynn. *First Lady from Plains*. Boston: Hougton Mifflin, 1984.

Eisenhower, Julie Nixon. *Pat Nixon: The Untold Story*. New York: Simon and Schuster, 1986.

Ford, Betty. *The Times of My Life*. New York: Harper and Row, 1978.

Johnson, Lady Bird. *A White House Diary*. New York: Holt, Rinehart and Winston, 1970.

Moore, Virginia. *The Madisons*. New York: McGraw-Hill, 1979.

Reagan, Nancy. *My Turn: The Memoirs of Nancy Reagan*. New York: Random House, 1989.

Roosevelt, Eleanor. *Autobiography of Eleanor Roosevelt*. New York: Barnes and Noble Books, 1978.

Russell, Francis. *The Shadow of Blooming Grove: Warren G. Harding in His Times*. New York: McGraw-Hill, 1968.

Taft, Helen Herron. *Recollection of Full Years*. New York: Dodd, Mead, 1914.

Thayer, Mary V. *Jacqueline Kennedy: The White House Years*. Boston: Little, Brown and Company, 1971.

Turner, Justin and Linda. eds. *Mary Todd Lincoln: Her Life and Letters*. New York: Alfred A. Knopf, 1972.

INDEX

Photo Credits

Photographs courtesy of Gerald R. Ford Library: pp. 6, 118, 124, 125, 127; Library of Congress, pp. 10, 14, 15, 20, 23, 27, 29, 35, 40, 48, 145; The Pennsylvania Academy of Fine Arts, Philadelphia, Harrison Earl Fund, p. 16; Free Library of Philadelphia, p. 19; Illinois State Historical Library, 30, 32, 34, 38; Craig Schermer, pp. 44, 56, 58, 61, 62, 64, 65, 68; Cincinnati Historical Society, 47, 54; Franklin D. Roosevelt Library, 73, 76, 77, 79, 81 (both); John F. Kennedy Library, pp. 84, 91, 95, back cover; Richard Morgan, p. 86; Lyndon Baines Johnson Library, pp. 96, 99, 102, 103; Wardman Library, Whittier College, pp. 109, 110, 112; National Archives, pp. 115, 117; Jimmy Carter Library, 130, 133, 138, 140; Bill Fitz-Patrick, The White House, p. 142; Office of Presidential Libraries / National Archives, pp. 146, 151, 152.